THE GREEN BIRD

THE GREEN BIRD

A Commedia Dell'Arte Play in Three Acts

by CARLO GOZZI

Translated and Adapted by

JOHN D. MITCHELL, Ed.D.
President,
Institute for Advanced Studies
in Theatre Arts

Consultant: Hugh A. Harter,
The Robert Hayward Professor,
Romance Languages,
Ohio Wesleyan University

NORTHWOOD INSTITUTE PRESS
Midland, Michigan 48640

First Edition

© 1985 by Northwood Institute Press

LCN 84-060780   ISBN 0-87359-040-6

Printed in the United States of America

DEDICATION

For my dear children, Barbarina and Renzo,
and to my beloved teacher of Italian, Eva Prina.

TABLE OF CONTENTS

ILLUSTRATIONS

by

Caissa Douwes

Born in Philadelphia in 1961, Caissa Douwes studied at Temple University and graduated with a BFA in painting from the Tyler School of Art. Miss Douwes spent a year in Rome and has had exhibits there as well as in Philadelphia. She is currently living in New York City where she is a free-lance artist and illustrator.

ACKNOWLEDGEMENTS

The Institute for Advanced Studies in the Theatre Arts is deeply indebted to Giovanni Poli, the master director who came from Venice to direct American professional actors in the production of THE GREEN BIRD (L'Augellin Belverde). Giovanni Poli, as well, and his wife Carla have been central to the realization of this *commedia dell'arte* text in English translation and in the original Italian and Venetian dialect. Giovanni took the writer and his American actors into this bright and lyrical world of *commedia*. He was an ebullient and exacting task-master, which resulted in all coming to know the style of this unique form of Italian theatre. Giovanni was more than Italian, he was Venetian. Both he and Carla became the dearest of friends and ever supportive of the work in theatre and films of the Institute for Advanced Studies in the Theatre Arts. The warmest and most heartfelt thanks are due to Carla Poli and to Eva Prina, for they became an essential key to unlocking the meaning of Venetian words and phrases.

A very special thanks and indebtedness is due Professor Hugh A. Harter of Ohio Wesleyan University whose eagerness to join forces with the writer resulted in contributing invaluable suggestions, verses, and phrasing. His vast knowledge of the Romance Languages had ever been a spur to the writer's ambitions.

C. George Willard's association with THE GREEN BIRD has been a very long one, and his love of the play as a theatre piece has never waivered. His friendship and working association with the writer has spanned two decades.

The writer wishes to acknowledge certain friends and colleagues who have contributed richly to this book and to whom I am indebted for their continuous encouragement and enthusiasm: Professor Giovanna Dompe; George Drew; Judith Elder, who had seen the work of Giovanni Poli and his troupe at the International Theatre Festival in Paris and had called to the attention of the Institute for Advanced Studies in the Theatre Arts this unique master of the style of *commedia dell'arte*; Robert Epstein; Edward P. Godek, Jr.; Mary W. John; Paul Joseph; Count Alvise Memmo; Angie Mitchell; William

Mitchell; Poet William Packard; Frank Rowley; and Nina Savo.

Thanks are due to Gil Forman and to Irene Shawtell who saw the project through from inception to completion.

The writer also wishes to thank Dr. David E. Fry, President of Northwood Institute, and Drs. R. Gary Stauffer and Arthur E. Turner of Northwood Institute for their commitment to the book. Heartfelt thanks are due, as well, to Virginia Morrison of Northwood Institute for her editorial assistance and creativity.

A theatre piece is more than literature and it only truly comes alive when it is onstage brought to life by actors. In the crucible of rehearsal and presentation of THE GREEN BIRD the following actors contributed invaluable insights that shaped the final translation: Wayne Adams, Wil Albert, Peter Blaxill, Margaret Blohm, William Burdick, Lauro Canales, Andra Carvino, Lynda Chapin, Harold Cherry, Julia Curry, Stephen Daley, Anita Dangler, Edgar Daniels, Jenny Dowling, Joan Dubrow, Stan Dworken, Rex Eckley, Jack Eddleman, Allene Elliot, Craig Elliot, Eileen Frank, Avril Gentles, Joseph Giovinazzo, George Gitto, Barry Alan Grael, Carol Guilford, Jacqueline Hand, Delphi Harrington, Sam Haigler Henry, Molly Hoover, Henry Horwege, Carl Jacobs, Don Jamison, Bella Jarrett, Jim Johnson, Charlotte Jones, Laurence Kabat, Kay Kingston, Elaine Knight, James Krueger, Miller Lide, Glen Lincoln, Ray Lonergan, my wife Miriam Mitchell, Richard Morse, Joe Narvid, Nina Polan, Don Reiker, Natalie Ross, Raymond St. Jacques, Dorothy Sands, Eric Tavares, Fiddle Viracola, Frank Vohs, Ron Weiss, Elaine Winters, and Arne Zaslove.

INTRODUCTION

THE GREEN BIRD by Carlo Gozzi is a companion piece to its
Chinese counterpart, THE FOX CAT SUBSTITUTED FOR THE
CROWN PRINCE, a Peking opera set in the Song Dynasty. THE
GREEN BIRD *(L'Augellin Belverde)* of Carlo Gozzi is the last of his ten
fairy tale plays *(fiabe)*. It is considered his masterpiece. Its' premier
was at the Teatro San Samuele, Venice on January 19, 1975.

Count Carlo Gozzi (1720-1806) came from an old patrician family
of Venice. At the age of twenty-seven, he began to show his artistic
bent and his conservatism. He took part in the founding of an academy
made up of reactionary intellectuals determined to "restore the purity
of the language (Tuscan Italian and Venetian dialects) undermined by
the innovations of Francophiles."*

Gozzi's theatrical concepts, like his political views took root in the
traditional past, *commedia dell'arte.* Stock situations and stock
characters were bases for *commedia.* Performances had a spontaneous quality, for popular actors interrupted the plot development with
impromptu gags, contemporary references, and clownish routines. It
was fast, bright, noisy theatre with little intellectual appeal.

Gozzi deplored and roundly denounced the contemporary Venetian theatre of playwrights Carlo Goldoni and Pietro Chiari. Both
these playwrights provoked the conservative Gozzi to satire and attack. Goldoni's reply is reportedly to have been, pointing to his
attendance figures and the box office returns, that it is one thing to
criticize, quite another to write a play that would draw the crowds.
Gozzi met the challenge; he wrote out, as was the practice in *commedia dell'arte,* a scenario of thirty one pages and this is titled THE
LOVE OF THREE ORANGES *(L'Amore Delle Tre Melerance);* some
small part of this first script of Gozzi is dialogue. The balance of the
text is synopses of action, springboards from which the actors impro-
vised. Gozzi's first play presented by a famous *commedia dell'arte*
troupe at the Teatro San Samuele, Venice, was a triumph. Gozzi's
tenth fairy tale play, THE GREEN BIRD, was in the nature of a sequel to

---

*Toscanini, W. "New faces for old faces", *Opera News,* Vol. 25; Number 17; Mar. 4,
1961.

xiii

THE LOVE OF THREE ORANGES. The Princess Ninetta, who had been immured in one of the three oranges and survived, is the Queen Ninetta of the latter play.

Gozzi went from strength to strength taking his work more seriously; he chose to write out more fully his subsequent nine *fiabe*.

The free, but routinized, vulgarly familiar *commedia dell'arte* enabled Gozzi to successfully satirize and attack his fellow playwrights. Carlo Goldoni beat a retreat and went into exile in Paris.

Goldoni's humanism *had* been more to the Italian taste and, although a successful playwright who had started with *commedia dell'arte*; e.g. his THE SERVANT OF TWO MASTERS (*Arlecchino Servitore di due Padroni*), he had broken with traditional Italian theatre and had made dramatic history by pushing drama in the direction of realism, credible people and everyday situations.

Gozzi wrote for a *commedia dell'arte* troupe headed by Giovanni Antonio Sacco, a famous Arlecchino. The fourth of his plays, TURANDOT (1762) is his most famous, which despite the story's being set in China is a tale from a Persian novel. Gozzi's literary and scholarly brother, Gasparo (1713-86) was the likely person to have called to Carlo Gozzi's attention exotic stories from the Middle East and Far East. Among Gossi's plays is THE LADY SERPENT (*La Donna Serpente*), which has a plot strikingly similar to the Chinese tale out of that country's folklore, known as THE WHITE SNAKE (*Bai She Jian*). In recent times it has become one of the most popular of Peking operas.

In both the Peking opera and in Gozzi's play, the plot relates how a snake goddess had transformed herself into a mortal woman in order to experience earthly love. Had the popular Chinese story come via the silk road to Venice, reaching the ears of Carlo Gozzi, inspiring him to write for his troupe of actors LA DONNA SERPENTE?

At the Teatro Eliseo, Rome, Italy, 1980, La Compagnia Stabile di Genova presented their production of Carlo Gozzi's LA DONNA SERPENTE in an eighteenth century style with sets and costumes by Luzzati inspired by Asian theatre.

"The fact that this trade route was secure meant that international contacts grew. Trade increased, as did cultural exchange and mutual visits. China exported various goods West, but mainly silk ... At that time many merchants came to China from the West to buy silk.**

Another characteristic of Gozzi's plays is his use of topical and local references. It creates something of a problem for today's producers of his plays. Apparently Carlo Gozzi thought of his plays as of his time and for his actors and his Venetian audiences. For example, in THE GREEN BIRD he makes reference not only to the Piazza San Marco but also to a gondolier by name, Cappello!

Carlo Gozzi's vogue did not last. However, in 1777-78, his works appeared in German. Lessing, Goethe, and Schiller (who reworked TURANDOT) were attracted to Gozzi's combination of magic, romanticism (to them), and robust humor.

Then, as the hold on theatre of realism loosened at the end of the nineteenth century, the plays of Gozzi came to be reevaluated in Italy and elsewhere. The Italian scholar, Ernesto Masi, praises Carlo Gozzi's *fiabe* as being among the glories of Italian literature.*

A goal in translating and adapting THE GREEN BIRD has been to make it available to readers in English as well as to provide a text for productions of the play. The original text is provided, as well, for study of Italian theatre and language.

The writer has come to think of the Chinese as the 'Italians' of Asia; just as he thinks of the Italians as the 'Chinese' of the Western World. THE GREEN BIRD and THE FOX CAT have the greatest similarity as examples of popular theatre of two greatly separated, geographically, countries. Each play mirrors the culture of its country of origin. The writer finds some striking cultural similarities reflected in the two plays; the writer is also very much aware that there are striking dissimilarities, culturally.

There is a strong parallel between THE GREEN BIRD and THE FOX CAT in that in both there is the ploy of substitution; likewise, in each of the two plays use is made of the supernatural. The Green Bird comforts and keeps alive the displaced Queen Ninetta; a supernatural and mythical character rescues Lady Li from the burning Palace of Disgrace where Lady Li had been put away. The supernatural elements and the places of incarceration in both narratives are parallels.

**Myrdal, Jan, *The Silk Road*, New York: Pantheon Books, (c.1979)

*Masi, Ernesto. *Fiabe di Carlo Gozzi*, Vol. I, II. Bologna, Zanichelli, 1885.

Brighella, as a villain at court in league with Dowager Queen Tartagliona, suggests comparison with the evil and powerful eunuch the Imperial Court, Guo Huai, in league with Lady Liu in the Peking opera.

The minister, Pantalone (a masked character as is Brigella) plays a role in saving the life of the twins, Renzo and Barbarina. In THE FOX CAT a eunuch, Chen Lin, high in the imperial court takes charge of saving the baby Crown Prince. In the Italian play, puppies were substituted for the twins; a tailess wild cat was submitted for the baby in THE FOX CAT. In each play there are foster parents and children adopted by foster parents. In THE FOX CAT, Lady Di becomes foster mother to Fan Zhonghua. Eighth-one-thousand-year-old and his wife, Lady Di, are foster parents to the Crown Prince born to Lady Li; in THE GREEN BIRD, Truffaldino and Smeraldina have become foster parents of the twins, Renzo and Barbarina.

The dowager Queen Mother, Tartagliona dominates her son, Tartaglia, the King. He in turn is childish. Both the Emperors in THE FOX CAT are dominated by Queen Lady Liu. Neither Emperor seems very bright. These are parallels.

What seems today like striking modernity is Carlo Gozzi's satirizing, in dowager Queen Tartagliona, mothers and mothers-in-law. Mothers in the Italian family are said to be the 'power behind the throne.' Gozzi makes of Queen Tartagliona a figure of fun. Here one comes upon a marked cultural difference in the two plays, for it is unthinkable in a Chinese tale or drama that a grandmother would do away with her grandchildren.

Likewise the Confucian dictum of filial piety has ever been strong in China. The absence of filial piety in THE GREEN BIRD would be unthinkable in a Peking opera; for example, Barbarina's and Renzo's leaving the home of their foster parents and, later, Barbarina's treatment of her foster mother Smeraldina would not occur in a chinese narrative.

Returning to cultural similarities, the playwright Gozzi knew his popular Italian audience. He could not resist, even in the tragic displacement of the Queen Ninetta, getting laughs through impresoning her under the toilets. Chinese and Italians share in language and comedic actions frank acceptance of biological functions. Each seems to delight in scatological humor.

The masked character Truffaldino refers to his heart by placing his hand on an appliqued heart on the seat of his pants. His language is crude and outspoken and is scatological. Bluntness of language for laughs from popular audiences exists in Peking opera; e.g. THE FOX CAT.

In view of Carlo Gozzi's story choices it seems likely that he had become aware of the Chinese tale as it evolved by the Qing Dynasty, an era parallel to his own 18th century. Of the 26 books about Carlo Gozzi researched in the specialized Theatrical Library, Trastevere, Rome, all agree that the material for Gozzi's *fiabe* came from two sources: folkloric and Oriental. Professor Giovanna Dompe of Rome is convinced that the inspiration for THE GREEN BIRD was Chinese. Thus it seems likely that the story that evolved from the time of the Song Dynasty and later became known in the Qing Dynasty as the Peking opera THE FOX CAT SUBSTITUTED FOR THE CROWN PRINCE had been the catalyst that triggered the imagination of Carlo Gozzi to write THE GREEN BIRD.

The full text, as printed, of Carlo Gozzi's L'AUGELLIN BELVERDE *(The Green Bird)* is longer than this adaptation and is in a five act version. Due to *canovacci*, for improvisation, it is incomplete as a text. Giovanni Poli, a man of the theatre, a scholar and, most important, a Venetian, fleshed out the text for performance in modern times. The adaptation of THE GREEN BIRD in English, with the restoration of two scenes from the Carlo Gozzi text, is much indebted to the adaptation fashioned by Giovanni Poli.

John D. Mitchell

COMMEDIA DELL'ARTE

The first Italian actors wearing masks go back to Ancient Rome. There was a type of theatre called 'Attellan' with four stock masked actors: Pappus, an old man; Maccus, a stupid servant; Bucco, a servant with a wide mouth; and Dossennus, a sly hunchback. Some characters, particularly servants, in the plays of the Roman dramatist Plautus recalled the 'Attellan' theatre.

There seems to be a lack of documents relating specifically to the *commedia dell'arte* during the late Roman Empire and in the Middle Ages. Actors wearing masks reappear, in a different form, only during the Renaissance. These masked characters, *maschere*, are the *zannis*, characters similar to the 'Attellan' Bucco; the appellation *zannis* comes from Giovanni (Giovanni-Gianni-Zanni).

They are the hungry fellows who came from the region of Bergamo, traveling to Venice in search of work, and usually ending up carrying coal. In addition to being servants carrying coal, the *zannis* exercise a less tiring profession, that of 'go-between.' The *zannis* of the 17th century had become the new familiar stylized masked characters, *maschere*. The patches of their costumes had now assumed a regular lozenge shape and their gait had a dance-like rhythm. The *zanni* had now evolved into the character of Truffaldino. Realistic *zannis* had by now disappeared making way for the famous Italian masked character, Arlecchino. This change of appellation stems from the return to Italy of the famous 'Zan Ganassa', under the name of Arlequin, which the Parisians had pinned upon him in memory of a traditional, agile red devil. The scenarios of the *commedia dell'arte* had become highly comic. They deal, for the most part, with simple situations, told in an irreverent manner.

Among the successors to the group of *zanni* characters is the old Pantalone (the name now given to the 16th century Magnifico). Brighella is another *zanni* character who evolved out of the urbane life of Venice; in his domesticated state, he becomes a faithful major domo. Arlecchino, on the other hand, had retained much of his original 16th century character, being primitive, spontaneous, and rebellious. Inevitably in scenarios he clashed with Brighella, and they beat each other up. Only in the 18th century was Arlecchino raised by the playwright, Carlo Goldoni, to a higher level; he was allowed to take off his mask and fall in love. In so doing, however, he lost much of his original identity and became a person like any other. It cannot be categorically stated that Carlo Goldoni brought about the end of *commedia dell'arte*, for in his time it was already in a state of decay. Goldoni did give to the *commedia dell'arte*, as a poet, a higher literary form and themes and characters out of every day life, and even in certain so called 'reform' comedies of Goldoni the influence and the vitality of *commedia dell'arte* endures.

The defense of the old *commedia dell'arte* and it's flights of fancy became the themes of Gozzi's plays. In his fairytale-like plays *(fiabe)* the *maschere* and the traditional and fantasy returned to the stages of Venice.

Contemporary clowns may be different in appearance, but their essential nature is that of the masked characters of the *commedia dell'arte*. Their stylized costumes and make-up, their exaggerated voice patterns and abstract broad gestures, the musical rhythm of their dance movements clearly tell us that the clowns and comedians of today constitute the *commedia dell'arte* of modern times. The 16th century *zanni* and their descendants in the 18th century, for example Arlecchino, became the successors of today's clowns.

LE PERSONE

BRIGHELLA, poeta ed indovino, finto amante di Tartagliona
PANTALONE, Ministro di Re Tartaglia
TRUFFALDINO, salsicciaio
SMERALDINA, sua sposa
BARBARINA
               / gemelli
RENZO
CALMON, antica statua morale, Re dei simulacri
NINETTA, moglie di Tartaglia e madre di Gemelli
AUGEL BELVERDE, Re di Terradombra, amante di Barbarina
TARTAGLIA, Re di Monterotondo
TARTAGLIONA, Vecchia Regina dei Tarocchi e madre di Tartaglia
POMPEA, statua amata da Renzo
FATA SERPENTINA
IL POMO CHE DANZA
L'ACQUA CHE BALLA
IL RE DI TERRADOMBRA
GLI ALBERI, I SOLDATI, I MORI

THE CHARACTERS

(as they appear)

BRIGHELLA, the court astrologer
PANTALONE, the Prime Minister
TRUFFALDINO, a shopkeeper
SMERALDINA, his wife
BARBARINA)
)
RENZO) twins, their adopted son
)
) and daughter
CALMON, a statue of a philosopher
NINETTA, the Queen, wife of Tartaglia
THE GREEN BIRD, a dancer
TARTAGLIA, the King
TARTAGLIONA, the Queen, his mother
POMPEA, a statue of a princess
FATA SERPENTINA, an offstage singer
THE APPLE, a singer
THE WATER, six dancers
KING OF TERRADOMBRA, The Bird transformed
  Soldiers of Tartaglia)
)
  Servants of the Twins)
) ...(Mimes)
  Enchanted Trees)
)
  Monsters)

1

L'Augellin Belverde

PROLOGO

(Musica e via le luci di sala, lentamente. Il sipario è chiuso. Da destra esce in proscenio Brighella, che viene illuminato da un solo proiettore.)

Brighella

O sol, che ti xe specchio
de le umane vicende,

(Da sinistra, illuminato da un proiettore, esce Pantalone.)

mai ti diventi vecchio
per scoprir a chi sa cose tremende!

Pantalone

Mi ghe son mato drio sto poeta. El dixe cose, che le xe da retraser; el fa versi, che i xe per raccolta per nozze.

Brighella

O dei Tarocchi misera regina!
O Tartaglia felice!
O Renzo, o Barbarina!
Tal frutto nasce da fatal radice!

Pantalone

Olè! Qua L'entra in tel sangue real de Monterotondo. La regina dei Tarocchi meschina? Sior si; la se lo merita. Sta vecia marantega dopo la partenza del re Tartaglia, so fio, no la fa altro che tiranie, e lu no

THE GREEN BIRD

PROLOGUE

(The act curtain is closed. The theatre is dark. BRIGHELLA suddenly appears at proscenium left, lighted by a spotlight. From stage right, PANTALONE appears in front of the act curtain, and he is lighted by a spotlight. PANTALONE comments on the predictions of BRIGHELLA.)

BRIGHELLA

Sun, you are like a mirror and show
The varied deeds of human kind;
You are not yet too old to glow
With the terrible happenings you find!

PANTALONE

This poet drives me out of my mind. He's always saying things he has to take back later. His verses should end up on an outhouse wall.

BRIGHELLA

Oh wretched, woeful Tarot Queen!
You Tartaglia, oh happy King!
Such fruit that comes from root unclean,
Of Barbarina and of Renzo sing!

PANTALONE

Ole, now it comes: the royal blood of the Monterotondo. He says the Queen of Tarots is a wretch! Yes, Sir! She deserves that. That hag! After her son, King Tartaglia left for the war, she became a tyrant.

BRIGHELLA

Tartaglia, King whom I so clearly see!
Back to the court now you have come,

Pantalone

merita de essere felice per aver lassà el governo in man per el corso de disdot'anni a sta striga. Fussela morta da quel resipiglion che la gaveva in te le gambe al tempo de le nozze de so fio. Mi no capisso. O Renzo, o Barbarina! Tal frutto nasce da fatal radice!

Brighella

Tartaglia ti vedo;
tu torni alla corte;
Ninetta, nol credo,
non sei fra le morte,
non son perse ancora le speranze.
discendenza real delle Naranze.

Pantalone

No ghe'e caso, bisogna star co la bocca verta, e ascoltarlo, come cocali.

(Durante la seguente battuta, il sipario, ad un movimento di magia di Brighella, si apre lentamente.)

Tartalgia te vedo? el re Tartagia che xe andà alla querra contro i ribelli, e che xe disnov'anni ch'el manca, xe qua stassera seguro

(Un gioco di luci che fa apparire, attraverso il sipario trasparente, la reggia di Tartaglia, l'esercito regio in ordine di partenza e a lato Tartaglia a cavallo di un asino. Entra in scena Tartagliona che abbraccia il figlio; anche Ninetta abbraccia Tartaglia, il quale — con un gesto grottescamente e comicamente eroico — alza la spada e dà l'ordine di partenza. L'esercito si mette in marcia ed esce, seguendo il re; Tartagliona e Ninetta salutano con la mano, braccio proteso.)

(PANTALONE)

Anyone like Tartaglia who left the government for eighteen long years in the hands of this witch doesn't deserve to be happy. I wish she had died when she had that rash on her legs at the time of her son's wedding. I don't understand it! "Oh, Renzo! Oh, Barbarina! Such fruit that from a fatal root was born!"

BRIGHELLA

Tartaglia, King whom I so clearly see!
Back to the court now you have come;
Ninetta, I can't believe that this could be,
That you to death could yet succomb.
And so all hope is not yet dead,
You who from Naranze blood was bred.*

PANTALONE

All one can do is to stand with mouth open, like a gull and listen to him.

> (BRIGHELLA, as if by magic, with a wave of his hand, causes the act curtain to open.)

PANTALONE

Is that you I see, Tartaglia? King Tartaglia who went to war against the rebels, and was missing for nineteen years, is here tonight for certain?

> (During BRIGHELLA's and PANTALONE's dialogue, the royal palace of TARTAGLIA has appeared. On the following long speech of PANTALONE, the following pantomime takes place: KING TARTAGLIA kisses goodby to NINETTA--fanfare--and with his army, made up of six mimes, leaves for the war. Soldiers march; NINETTA cries; TARTAGLIONA chases

---

*A reference to the earlier play, L'amore delle Tre Melarance (The Love of Three Oranges) by Carlo Gozzi, of which L'augellin Belverde is a sequel.

(Ninetta esce, scacciata da Tartagliona. Ninetta entra in scena con due gemelli neonati; Tartagliona glieli strappa e li consegna a Pantalone. Tartagliona chiama col gesto due soldati che afferrano Ninetta, la incatenano e la rinserrano nel "buco della scaffa", che appare dietro la reggia, la quale si apre e si richiude. Soldati e Tartagliona escono di scena.)

Pantalone

Ninetta, no ti è fra le morte? Oh, qua no ghe la catto. La regina Ninetta xe stada seppelia viva, xe disdot'anni, sotto el buso de la scaffa per le persecuzion de sta vecia carampia de regina, e l'ho vista mi co sti occhi. Figurarse, se no la se marcia, e in polvere? No xe persa la discendensa delle Naranze? L'è bella! Ma no le se pol sorbir. Se me par che sia ancora quel momento fatal che la quondam povera regina Ninetta, prima de esser sepolta viva sotto el buso della scaffa, ha partorio quei do zemelli putello e putella, che gera un naroncolo e una riosa de belleza. A mi i me xe stai consegnai da sta vecchia carampia de so nono coll'ordene de scannarli e, pena la mia vita, de taser. E me par ancora de veder l'azion negra de metter in te la cuna, in cambio dei do zemelli, do cagnetti mufferle, che aveva partorito la Mascherina de Corte; scrivendo po al re quelle relazion, quelle accuse, quelle iniquità che ha causà tanti ordeni tragici, i quali sarà cintai sotto al camin, come fiabe. Xe ben vero, che mi no ho abuo cuor de scannar quelle raise e me recordo, come se fusse in sto punto, che li ho fatti in rodolo con ventiquattro brazze de tela incerada veneziana, perfetta, de quella del Buso, e che con la possibile diligenza ben condizionai per difenderli dall'umiditae, ho buttà quel caro tramesso zozo per el fiume, portando a so nona do cuori de cavretto, come sol far i boni ministri in sti casi. Dopo disdott'anni, se anca no i xe morti negai, o dalla fame, i sarà morti per no aver podesto crescer, perchè so de averli cussì stretti col spago sforzin. Sior strolego caro, se' un poeta felice, no se' imitator, no affettè la lingua toscana; le vostre xe cose e non parole; el ciel sa dar el gran

NINETTA out of the palace; NINETTA returns with the twins and rocks them in her arms; TARTAGLIONA grabs the twins, NINETTA cries; TARTAGLIONA orders two soldiers to chain NINETTA's hands and feet and they take her out; TARTAGLIONA gives PANTALONE the twins; PANTALONE wraps twins.)

PANTALONE

Ninetta, you are not among the dead? I'll not be fooled! Queen Ninetta was buried alive, eighteen years ago, in a hole under the toilets by order of the wretched old Queen Tartagliona. It seems to me I can still see it all again with my own eyes. So how can I believe that she's not rotted away and turned to dust? So the descendant of the Naranze is not lost? It would be wonderful! I can't believe it. I see it all again; that fatal moment when poor Queen Ninetta, before being buried alive under sewers, gave birth to twins, a boy and a girl, a buttercup and a beautiful rose. The old witch gave them to me and ordered me to kill them, and on pain of death, to keep silent. How I recall that black deed still! The bitch mascot of the court had had two puppies, and they were put in the cradle in place of the twins. She wrote all to the King, accusations, bad deeds, the causes of so many tragic happenings. One day all this will be recounted by the fireplace like some kind of a fable. True, I didn't have the heart to kill those twins. I remember it as if it were right now; to protect them from dampness, I wrapped them in twenty-four yards of Venetian waxed linen from the Buso shop on the Rialto. I tied them with twine, and then threw the dear bundle into the canal. I took to the grandmother two lambs' hearts, as good ministers were wont to do. I'd laugh in your face if the twins were not dead after eighteen years; dead of hunger, or maybe just dead because there was no way to grow up, so tightly I had wrapped them together. My dear astrologer, be a happy poet, don't be a fake, don't use schoolbook Italian.* Make your deeds more than just words, for heaven has given

---

*Pantalone has been speaking in Venetian dialect; the Italian of Tuscany, Dante's Italian, became and is today the accepted Italian of all Italy.

Pantalone

talento ai omeni, ma 'sti omeni sa anca dir delle bestialità de riderghe in tel muso. No gh'è più tacconi, la descendenza delle Naranze xe estinta.

Brighella

(Durante la battuta, lentamente sparisce la reggia di Tartaglia e appaiono la bottega di Truffaldino salumaio e il mare.)

Se dai tremendi pomi che cantano,
dall'acque d'oro che suonano e ballano,
dai re pennuti che cantano,

Tartaglina non sei difesa
per quella forza non unquanco intesa,
hai contrari simulacri
solidi, fluvidi, alcalici ed acri;
una pozzanghera sarà il tuo nicchio;
nè può difenderti
Brighella, strologo, vate Caicchio.
Ma, oimè, va mancando l'entusiasmo celeste; resto un minchion come tutti gli altri omeni. Me chiappa al solito languor de polmoni, me vien el consueto svenimento. Vedo vicina una bottega de luganegher. Reparemo co do soldi de sguazzeto la debolezza che sol lassar l'estro divin, el furor poetico.

(Entra nel negozio di Truffaldino.)

Pantalone

Sangue della Noffia che ha buo el terzo in regata! Che bel pezzo de poesia che xe sta questo. No ghe n'ho inteso una maledetta; porlo esser più divin de cussi? Pomi che cantano, acque che ballano, solidi, fluvidi, alcalici ed acri. Sia come che se voggia, qualcossa de grande ha da nascer de certo in sta Corte . . . No me stupisso de gnente; se pol dar tutto, se pol dar tutto.

(Esce di scena alla sinistra.)

great talent to men. Your lack of it prompts me to say bullshit and laugh right in your mutt. This is no joke: descendants of the Naranze are all extinct!

> (During the following, BRIGHELLA walks upstage, which by now has been transformed into a street with a shop and the sea in the background.)

BRIGHELLA

From apples that sing,
Golden waters projected,
   for your power is unequal.
From that Bird King feathered.
Tartagliona, you are not to be protected.
Your astrological signs, those solids: fluids, alkalines,
   acids, have not weathered.
A puddle will be your refuge, Your Grace!
You cannot be saved
By Brighella, your astrologer, from this disgrace.

BRIGHELLA

But, alas, heavenly enthusiasm fails me, I'm just as much a simpleton as everybody else. I can hardly breathe, I am so hungry. I feel faint. I see a sausage shop nearby. With my two cents, I'll restore my divine inspiration and poetic frenzy.

> (BRIGHELA enters the shop of TRUFFALDINO.)

PANTALONE

Pig's blood! You'd think he had placed third in the Venice Regatta. What a beautiful piece of poetry that is! I don't understand a damned word of it. What poet would write about apples that sing, waters that dance; solids, fluids, alkalines and acids? Come what may, something is bound to happen in this court. Nothing surprises me; it is just possible to believe everything, is possible to believe everything.

> (Exits.)

Tempo I
Scena I

(Da destra entra acrobaticamente Truffaldino, seguito da Smeraldina.)

Truffaldino

No la poss pï suppurtà; prima che i la brusass, l'era 'na femena mata che servia a qualcossa, ma se savea de resuscitar 'na minciona, l'avarae lassà cenere e carbon. Maledeto co l'ho vista sta femena malcreaa . . .

Smeraldina

Molto, molto meglio certamente sarebbe stato che io fossi rimasta cenere e carbone piuttosto che sposare un bricone della tua risma, che non pensa altro che mangiare e dilapidare in vizi i capitali della bottega.

Truffaldino

Senti che bocca descusìa. No la dis miga che el cavedal l'ho vandagnà mi, col sudor della fronte, fasendo el cogo a corte . . .

Smeraldina

. . . rubando a corte . . .

Truffaldino

Siora no, siora no, mi non ho rubà, sior muso da slepe. Ho solo sgrafignà onestaminte, come fa tuti i coghi de reputazion; mejo averli butai in t'un foss i me vadagni, piutosto de averzer 'na botega de luganegher e che vu donassi a le comare tripe, luganeghe, brisiole e straculi . . .

ACT I
SCENE I

(A street with wing flats as houses at both sides of stage and a ground row sea in back. TRUFFALDINO, SMERALDINA chase each other.)

TRUFFALDINO

I can't stand her anymore; before I burned her up, she was a woman, useful for something; but had I known better than to revive this simpleton, I would have left her to be coal and ashes.* Cursed be the day that I saw this rude woman...

SMERALDINA

Much, much better certainly it would have been if I had remained ashes and coal rather than marry the world's biggest scoundrel who thinks of nothing but eating and squandering on his vices all the goods of our shop.

TRUFFALDINO

Listen to that foul-mouth. She doesn't admit that I earned the money I spent with the sweat of my brow, a cook at the court.

SMERALDINA

...stealing from the palace kitchens!

TRUFFALDINO

No, signora! No, signora! I did not steal signora, you pigsnout! I just pilfered as honestly as any cook of good repute. I would have alone been better to have thrown all I earned down a well, rather than open a salami shop to see you dole out sausage, tripe, bologna and liver-wurst! And all for nothing!

*A reference to *Love of Three Oranges*.

13

Smeraldina

Piano, piano. Fui un po' facile ma posso protestare davanti al cielo di esserlo stato per bon di cuore; d'altra parte sono stata sempre in utile al negozio, ma tu dimentichi quello che hai mangiato a tutte le ore, mettendoti sino sotto al capezzale il fegato fritto da mangiare alla notte.

Truffaldino

Olà, scagassera! Chi ha fato credensa ai fachini, ai viturini, e ai garzoni?

Smeraldina

Svergognato! E quello che hai sperperato nelle osterie con i tuoi degni amici?

Truffaldino

La gh'ha un cervello co fa una galina. La gh'ha
imprestà soldi parfin ai poeti . . .

Smeraldina

Soldi ne sono andati molti, sì, ma per le femene di mal odore che tu frequentavi, in danno non solo della bottega ma anche di te medesimo, perchè ho dovuto poi dare a medici, speziali e chirurghi prosciutti, bondole, salsicce e salami.

Truffaldino

Mo' la gran lengua, sta cagabessi! La vul semper parlar ela! Intanto in

SMERALDINA

Easy there, easy! I may have been a little easy-going, but I can swear to God I was like that because I'm goodhearted; but on the other hand I have always been useful about the shop, but you lie about what you ate at each and every hour, even hiding fried liver under your pillow, to eat in the night.

TRUFFALDINO

Ola! You old shit,* giving credit to porters, to coachmen, to waiters!

SMERALDINA

You're shameless! What about the money you threw away in taverns, squandering it on your "worthy" friends?

TRUFFALDINO

(To audience.)

Smeraldina has the brains of a chicken! Lending money — to — poets.

SMERALDINA

Money has been spent, lots of it. Yes, but you on your stinking whores. A drain on the shop, and a risk to your health! Afterwards, I had to pay the doctors, the druggists, the surgeons with hams, sausages *and* salamis!

TRUFFALDINO

Ha! With such a big tongue, you should shit money!** How she talks.

*The Venetian dialect word is equivalent to French slang *emmerdeuse*, cf. *merde*. (Carla Poli)

***Cagabessi* in Venetian dialect is equivalent to: *cacare denari*. (Carla Poli)

Truffaldino

botega no gh'è che quatro tolpi duri e do grossi de bisato e mi son andà in rovina per el bon cor de 'na mata. Pensar che l'ha voluo rancurar do puteli, trovai in tel fiume involtolai in t'una tela incerada, slatarli e deventar magra co fa'na sardela.

Smeraldina

Non toccarmi ne Renzo nè Barbarina . . .

Truffaldino

Da quel zorno no ti m'ha volù pì ben, e l'è questa propri la razon che m'ho svià da le teneresse matrimoniali . . .

Smeraldina

Ah! . . . per questa causa cercavi le femmine di malo odore!

Truffaldino

Cercavo de solevarme l'anema da le bestialità de voler mantegnir un putelo e 'na putela fin a l'età de disdot'anni.

Smeraldina

Ti ripeto di non toccarli nè con fatti nè con parole altrimenti ti farò il diavolo a quattro.

Scena II

(Entrano Renzo e Barbarina, l'uno con un fucile da caccia, l'altra con un cesto di biancheria.)

Truffaldino

Li tocarò co una pedada in tel da drio. I xe stai la razon de la me rovina. In casa mia no li vogio più!

(TRUFFALDINO)

Now in the shop there is nothing but four hard sausages and two big eels. I'm a ruined man. I'm too goodhearted; I've let a mad woman ruin me. To think, she took in two twins I found in the river, wrapped in waxed cloth. She breastfed them and became skinny as a sardine.

SMERALDINA

Don't say a thing about Renzo and Barbarina.

TRUFFALDINO

From that day on you didn't love me any more. That's why I left the bed but kept the board.

SMERALDINA

(Scornfully,)

Hah! So that's why you went for those stinking sluts!

TRUFFALDINO

I was trying to raise my spirits. Oh, the stupidity of having to provide for a boy and girl for eighteen years!

SMERALDINA

I tell you again: don't lay a finger on the twins. In deed or word, or I'll be worse than four devils.

SCENE II

(Enter Renzo and Barbarina: Renzo with a gun and a book; Barbarina with a basket of laundry.)

TRUFFALDINO

I'll not lay a finger on them; I'll give them a kick in the ass. They're the cause of my ruination. I don't want them in my home ever again.

Smeraldina

O cielo! Come puoi aver cuore di scacciare due figlioli così ob-
bedienti, buoni e indifferenti agli incomodi? Mangiano gli avanzi,
studiano sempre e per di più sono utili, perchè Renzo va a caccia e
reca sempre conigli e lepri, e Barbarina va a legna, lava e spazza.

Truffaldino

Bei vadagni! Barbarina con quel muso da santa peppa, cossa voleu
che la porta a casa? Maginarse Renzo co quell'aria da filosofo da
schiaffi. Mi no li voj pì veder.

Barbarina

Renzo, la madre nostra e il padre nostro sono in question.

Renzo

E' ver, deh, lo ascoltiam.

Smeraldina

Se avrai il coraggio di dire una parola torta a Renzo e a Barbarina farò
eccessi.

Truffaldino

Ho altro che coraio: no vedo l'ora che i torna per sbaterli fora de casa.

Smeraldina

Ti scongiuro, Truffaldino, non commettere una simile tirannia.

SMERALDINA

Oh heavens! How could you have the heart to send them away, two children so obedient, so good? So uncomplaining whatever the discomforts? They eat leftovers. They study all the time. They're useful. Renzo hunts and brings home rabbits and hares; Barbarina chops wood, does the laundry, sweeps the floor.

TRUFFALDINO

Humbug! Barbarina with the snout of a fake saint. What is she good for? And that Renzo with his air of a third-rate philosopher. I'll not have them around anymore.

BARBARINA

(Aside.)

Renzo, our mother and father are quarrelling.

RENZO

(Aside.)

Oh, yes. Pray let us listen.

SMERALDINA

If you dare to say one more word against Renzo or Barbarina, I'll not be responsible for what I do.

TRUFFALDINO

I'll do more than dare. Just wait! The minute they show themselves, I'll kick them out of the house.

SMERALDINA

Now, Truffaldino! You'll do no such thing!

Truffaldino

Mi no ho fioli e no voi far spese a bastardi.

Renzo

Bastardi siamo!

Barbarina

Io non intendo: come!

Smeraldina

Ti prego di non lasciarti mai scappar di bocca questa parola: bastardi!

Truffaldino

Xe disdott'anni che l'ho qua che la me soffega, ma adesso basta! Voi finalmente respirar; apena che i vien voj dirghe bastardi, bastardi mille volte bastardi!

Renzo

Padre! E' poi vero che siam bastardelli?

Barbarina

Ditemi, è ver che noi non vi siam figli?

Truffaldino

Bastardi!

Esce.

TRUFFALDINO

I have no children of my own. I'll not support two bastards.

RENZO

(Aside.)

We are Bastards!

BARBARINA

(Aside.)

I don't understand. How's that?

SMERALDINA

I beg of you, never again let fall that word from your lips: bastards!

TRUFFALDINO

For eighteen years I've had the word in my throat and it suffocates me. Now, it's enough. At last I can breathe. As soon as they return, I'll tell them to their faces. "Bastards! Bastards!" A thousand times: "Bastards!"

RENZO

Father, is it true that we are little bastards?

BARBARINA

Tell me, is it true that we are not your children?

TRUFFALDINO

Bastards!

(Exits.)

SCENA III

Renzo

Oh bella! Barbarina!
Ringrazio il ciel assai d'aver in sen richiuso
uno spirito forte.

Barbarina

Se i nostri libriccini filosofici
non avessimo letti, starei fresca.

Smeraldina

Cari miei figli, so che non darete
orecchio alcuno all'asino furfante
di mio marito.

Renzo

Ma siam vostri figli,
o no?

Smeraldina

No, non lo siete; ma che serve?
V'ho allattati, allevati come figli:
non dovete staccarvi dal mio seno.

Barbarina

No, Smeraldina.
Non è dover che chi del vostro sangue
non nacque, resti ad aggravar la vostra
famiglia meschinetta!

SCENE III

RENZO

How splendid, Barbarina!
I thank heaven for giving us
Strong hearts.

BARBARINA

If we hadn't studied our little books of philosophy,
We would be scared to death to be out in the cold.

SMERALDINA

My dear children; don't listen
To that ass of a husband
Of mine.

RENZO

Are we your children,
or not!

SMERALDINA

No, you're not, but does it matter?
I nursed you and raised you as my own children.
You cannot leave my bosom.

BARBARINA

No, Smeraldina.
It is not fitting that those who are not born of your blood
Should remain to aggravate
Your poverty-stricken family!

Barbarina

Io già tra me suppongo
che del distacco nostro voi proviate
qualche amarezza. Voi pensar dovete
che il dispiacere, che dentro a voi sentite,
nasce dall'amor proprio che in voi regna.

Smeraldina

Come amor proprio? Che parlare è questo?

Renzo

Brava sorella. Siete brava filosofa.
Mia cara Smeraldina. Ritiratevi, addio!

Barbarina

Ritiratevi, addio!

> (Renzo e Barbarina ridono, man mano aumentando d'inten-
> sita.)

Smeraldina

Per allattarvi mi svenai; spogliata
mi son per rivestirvi; dalla bocca
mi trassi il pane per nutrirvi insino
a questa età; per voi mille afflizioni,
mille angoscie ho sofferto; ed avrò fatto
tutto per amor proprio?

Renzo

Voi mi fate
rider di gusto, ah, ah, Si, certo,
per amor di voi stessa.

(BARBARINA)

I suppose that when we are gone,
You will feel
Some bitterness, but you must reflect
That the sorrow you feel
Is born of the self love that rules you.

SMERALDINA

Self love! What kind of talk is that!

RENZO

Fine, my sister! Your philosophy is very sound.
My dear Smeraldina, go back to your home. Bye-bye!

(Laughter.)

BARBARINA

Return to your home. Bye-bye!

(Laughter.)

SMERALDINA

To nurse you, I ruined my health.
To dress you, I gave up my clothes.
I denied myself bread to nourish you till now.
For you, I suffered a thousand afflictions,
A thousand pains. And all this
I did for love of myself?

RENZO

You really make me laugh!
Ah, yes, you certainly did it
For very love of yourself.

Smeraldina

O cielo!
dunque non ho con voi merito alcuno
di quanto feci?

Barbarina

Smeraldina, adagio.
L'intrinseco valore dell'azione
non vi da nessun merito.

Smeraldina

Io maledico
il punto in cui per troppo amar me stessa,
tanto ho penato ad allevar due ingrati,
due matti da legar che m'abbandonano
con tanta indifferenza e ingratitudine.
Se mai nessun più aiuto, che s'annega,
se mai vesto nessuno, ch'abbia freddo,
se mai più faccio un soldo d'elemosina,
a chi si muor di febbre o fame o sete,
poss'essere tenagliata, strangolata, tagliata
a pezzi, ed arsa un'altra volta.

(Esce.)

Scena IV

RENZO E BARBARINA

(Durante la battuta seguente, Renzo e Barbarina con passo
mimico si avviano verso il fondo della scena.
Dai lati lentamente escono le case. Solo nel fondo rimane il
mare.)

SMERALDINA

Oh, Heaven!
So I mean nothing to you?
After all I did for you!

BARBARINA

Smeraldina, easy now!
The intrinsic value of the action
Gives *you* no merit.

SMERALDINA

I curse
The moment in which for too much love of myself
I suffered so much to raise two ingrates.
Two raving lunatics who abandon me
With so much indifference and ingratitude.
If ever again I help anyone who needs help,
If ever I clothe anyone who is cold;
If I ever give a farthing of food
To anyone who is dying of fever, hunger, or thirst;
May I be pulled to pieces with pincers, strangled,
And cut in pieces and burned once again.*

SCENE IV

During this scene, BARBARINA and RENZO go with rhythmic
steps upstage toward the sea. In time to the rhythm of their
steps, the houses at both sides disappear one by one, until there
remains only the wild sea. (The sea is represented by a cut out
ground row.)

---

*A reference to The Love of Three Oranges.

Renzo

Ma questa è matta! Sorella,
scusar bisogna l'ignoranza.

Barbarina

E' vero!

Renzo

Ecco i computi
filosofici miei. Non abbiam padre,
non abbiam madre. Eccoci dunque sciolti
da obbedienza e soggezione.
Veniamo addesso
all'altro punto. Hai tu nessun amante?

Barbarina

No, in coscienza. Renzo, t'assicuro.

Renzo

Ne men io ho morose, ed ecco tronca
quella passion pericolosa
che infelici e ridicoli suol far
gli spasimanti.
E' questo un ben che supera di molto
il mal di questi stracci.
Spogliamoci d'amor proprio affatto, affatto,
e saremo felici. Andiam, sorella.

Barbarina

Odimi, Renzo. Io t'assicuro e giuro
che nessuno amerò, e sarò sempre
per la vita filosofa. Ma deggio

RENZO

Oh, she was mad! Sister,
Ignorance must be excused.

BARBARINA

It is true!

RENZO

Here are the results
Of my philosophical findings: we have no father,
We have no mother. Therefore, we are free
From obedience and bondage.
Let's come now
To the next point. Do you have a lover?

BARBARINA

No, in all conscience, Renzo, I assure you.

RENZO

Nor have I any sweethearts, and so we are cut off
From that dangerous passion
That makes lovers, racked with pain,
Unhappy and ridiculous.
This is a goodness much more important
Than the misfortune of these rags.
Let us shed ourselves of love of self completely,
And we shall be happy. Let's go, sister.

BARBARINA

Listen to me, Renzo. I assure you, and I swear
That I'll never fall in love; and I'll always be
For a life controlled by philosophy. But I must

Barbarina

confessarti però che spesso intorno
mi suol girare un certo Augel Belverde,
ch'egli mostra d'amarmi, e ch'io mi sento
per quell'animaletto alquanto debole.

Renzo

Nulla, sorella; io ti guarisco tosto
da quest'amor. Sappi, gli uccelli tutti,
per proprio istinto girano d'intorno
a tutte le civette. Quest'augello
ti crede una civetta e ti circonda.
Lungi da tutti andiamo, e fuor di questa
città pericolosa.

Barbarina

O mondo, o mondo!
certo sei tristo, se nemmen lusingar mi possa
dell'amicizia d'un Augel Belverde.

> (Renzo e Barbarina sono giunti sulla riva del mare. Insieme
> fanno un giro completo intorno a se stessi, lentamente, dando
> l'idea della vastità del mare.)

Barbarina

Renzo, la notte è presso: qui non vedo
che una spiaggia deserta. E' l'aer crudo;
e le piante e le mani e i denti in bocca
mi tremano dal freddo. Ti confesso,
l'amor proprio comincia a dominarmi.

Renzo

Barbarina, sta forte e lo sopprimi.
Io non mi reggo in piedi per la fame;

(BARBARINA)

Confess to you that often around me
Comes a certain Green Bird.
He flies around me as if to show that he loves me, and I feel
For that little bird some little weakness.

RENZO

It's nothing, sister; I'll immediately cure you
Of this love. You must know that all birds
By instinct fly
Around all flirts. This bird
Believes that you are a flirt and that's why he flies around you.
Let's go far away, and out of this
Dangerous city.

BARBARINA

Oh, world, world!
Certainly it's wicked if I cannot even rejoice
In the friendship of a small Green Bird.

> (They encircle the stage slowly, indicating the vastness
> of the sea.)

BARBARINA

Renzo, the night is falling. I see only
A deserted beach. The air is raw;
My feet, my hands and even the teeth in my mouth
Are shivering with cold. I must confess
That love of self is beginning to govern me.

RENZO

Be strong, Barbarina, and suppress it.
I can't stand on my feet, I'm so hungry.

Renzo

ma questa spiaggia ignuda d'ogni bene,
quest'essere lungi dagli uomini perfidi,
che tutto fan per amor proprio, credi,
mi rinfranca lo spirito . . .

Barbarina

Ma fratello,
se, verbigrazia, una persona adesso
ci invitasse all'albergo, ci accendesse
un bel foco d'inanzi, ci donasse
ben da cena, un buon letto; dimmi il vero,
questa persona ti rincrescerebbe?

Renzo

Avrei cara la cena, il foco, il letto;
ma quando riflettessi alla persona,
che solo per piacere a se medesima
ci darebbe l'alloggio, avrei rispetto
ad accettar quel beneficio.

Barbarina

Renzo, la fame, il freddo e la stanchezza
hanno in me tal vigor che agli occhi miei
ti dipingono un pazzo, ed un fanatico,
e pieno d'amor proprio più degli altri.

Scena V

(Tuono e lampi. Appare Calmon dalle acque e avanza. Barbarina si stringe al fratello.)

(RENZO)

But this beach, barren of any good,
Is far from perfidious men
Who do everything for love of self. Believe me,
It refreshes my spirit.

BARBARINA

But Brother,
For example, if right now a person
Invited us to an inn, lighted
Right before us a good fire, gave us
An excellent dinner, a good meal, tell me truly,
Would such a person prove displeasing to you?

RENZO

I would welcome the dinner, the fire, the bed,
But when I reflect upon the person,
I think that he would give us hospitality
Only to please himself, and I would hesitate
To accept that gift.

BARBARINA

Renzo, hunger, cold and sleep
Have so overcome me, that in my eyes
You are a nut and a fanatic
Full of love of yourself more than anybody else.

SCENE V

(Noise of wind, storm, etc. CALMON appears from the sea and advances. BARBARINA presses herself to her brother.)

Calmon

Barbarina ha ragion:
Renzo, apri gli occhi.

(Lampi e tuono. I due fratelli cadono a terra. Calmon **avanza**
verso di loro.)

Barbarina

O Dio. Renzo, una statua che parla!

Renzo

Dimmi, chi sei?

Calmon

Son un che giorno visse qual tu or sei
filosofo meschin. Scoprir pretesi
degli uomini l'interno, ed uomo anch'io
vidi amor proprio in tutti esser cagione
d'ogni menoma azion. Allor m'avenne
che pietra si fe'il cuor, le membra tutte
mi si cambiaro in marmo e nel terreno
caddi, ivi giacqui molt'anni fra l'erba
sepolto, e il sudiciume.

Renzo

Si, ma questo
non mi impedirà mai d'esser filosofo.

Calmon

Non te l'impedirò, ma nol sarai.

(Lampi e tuono.)

CALMON

Barbarina is right,
Renzo, open your eyes.

> (Lightning and thunder. The twins fall to earth. CALMON comes toward them.)

BARBARINA

Oh, God! Renzo, a statue that talks!

RENZO

Tell me, who are you?

CALMON

I am one who lived, as you do today,
An impish philosopher. I claimed
That I had discovered the inner man, and I also
Saw love of self as a reason
For every action in everybody
Then, my heart became stone. Every member of my **body**
Became marble, and I fell to the ground.
There I remained for many years,
Buried amidst grass and dirt.

RENZO

Yes, but this
Will never prevent me from being a philosopher.

CALMON

I will not oppose you, but you will not be one.

> (Lightning and thunder.)

Renzo

Alla fine, chi sei, e a che venisti?

Calmon

Fui re d'uomini un giorno, ora comando
a tutte le statue dei cimiteri.

(Lampi e tuono.)

Dagli avi vostri tratto fui dal fango
drizzato in un giardin della città
che vicina lasciaste.

Barbarina

Oh, cara statua! Dunque conoscesti
gli ascendenti di noi? Ci narra in grazia:
di chi siam figli? Tu devi saperlo.

Calmon

Lo so nè il posso dir. Dirò soltanto
che la dichiarazion dell'esser vostro
dipender de' dall'Augellin Belverde,

(Lampi e tuono.)

che gira intorno a Barbarina amante.
Quel sasso dinanzi a voi raccogliete;

(Lampi e tuono. Barbarina raccoglie il sasso.)

tornate alla città; là di rimpetto
alla reggia il scagliate, e di meschini
ricchi sarete tosto: a' gran perigli
Calmon chiamate. Vi domando solo
un picciol benefizio. A tempi andati

RENZO

Very well, who are you? Why do you come?

CALMON

I was once a king. Now I am in charge
Of all statues in cemeteries.

(Lightning and thunder.)

I was taken out of the mud by your ancestors,
Set up in a garden near to the city
You just left.

BARBARINA

Oh, dear statue! So you knew
Our ancestors? Please tell us;
Whose children are we? You must know.

CALMON

I know it, but that I cannot reveal. I will tell you only
That the revelation of who you are
Depends on the Green Bird.

(Lightning and thunder.)

Who, in love, flies around Barbarina.
Pick up that stone in front of you.

(Lightning and thunder
BARBARINA picks up the stone.)

Return to the city. Throw it opposite
The palace and at once you will go
From rags to riches. When in peril,
Call Calmon. I ask you only
A small favor. Some time ago,

Calmon

gl'insolenti fanciulli con le pietre
rotto m'aveano il naso. Un statuario
me lo rifece, ma questo al mio non somiglia:
io avevo naso aquilino. Procurate
ch'esso mi sia rifatto al mio conforme!
Amici addio!...

(Lampi e tuono.)

Renzo

Calmon, sorella, ci ha lasciati orfani,
pieni di fame, di freddo e di paura,
e con un sasso nelle mani. Oh caro!

Barbarina

Andiam, com'ei ci disse ed alla reggia
di rimpetto il scagliamo. Vederemo
le meraviglie da Calmon promesse,
dalle sciagure ch'ei ci ha minacciate,
forse usciremo, e alfin nelle miserie
siam fortunati, e lieti esser dobbiamo.

(I due fratelli escono.)

Scena VI

(Entra la scena della reggia di Tartaglia, la quale quindi si
apre, dando luogo al "buco della scaffa". Ninetta, singhioz-
zante, esce e si siede al centro del palcoscenico.)

Ninetta

Perchè mai vivo ancora, dopo sì lungo

(CALMON)

Naughty children broke my nose
With a stone. A sculptor
Made it over, but it doesn't look like my own:
I had an aquiline nose. Try
To have it made over as it was.
Friends, farewell!

> (Lightning and thunder.)
> (Exits.)

RENZO

Sister, Calmon has left us orphans,
Famished, freezing, afraid
With just a stone in our hands, Oh dear!

BARBARINA

Let's go and do as he told us. Let's throw
The stone in front of the Royal Palace. Let's see
The wonders that Calmon promised.
Maybe we'll be free
From misfortunes and miseries.
Oh, to be lucky and *have* to be happy.

> (They exit.)

SCENE VI

> (A pit under the washrooms. QUEEN NINETTA sits chained to
> a chair under the plumbing.)

NINETTA

Why am I still alive after so many years,

NINETTA

Here comes the ever sympathetic Green Bird.

Ninetta

tempo, sepolta in quest'orrida fossa,
dove tante immondizie, e si fetenti,
colano sempre? O di Concul figliuola,
mirabil Ninetta!
Ecco il pietoso usato Augel Belverde,
che di solito cibo mi soccorre,
pel buco della scafa discendendo.

> (Entra l'Augellin Belverde, il quale depone il cibo e fa una
> grottesca pantomima intorno a Ninetta. Quindi si pone ac-
> canto alla regina.)

O Augello, Augello, quanto meglio fora
il lasciarmi morir.

Augello

Ninetta, frena il pianto; forse non è lontano
il fin delle miserie e il sepolcro inumano.

Ninetta

Come? L'Augel Belverde che ragiona?

Augello

Non istupir, Ninetta.
Io son di Re figliuolo, e nell'età più verde
fui cambiato da un Orco in Augellin Belverde.
Sta la nostra fortuna, la nostra sorte ria,
in man di Barbarina, tua figlia e amante mia.

(NINETTA)

Buried down in this horrible pit,
Where so much dirt, so bad smelling,
Keeps draining!
O, Ninetta! Miserable daughter of King Concul!*
Here comes the ever sympathetic Green Bird,
Coming down through the hole of the toilets,
He saves me with the only food I get.

> (Enter GREEN BIRD, places the food, does a pantomime before
> NINETTA and takes up a place before NINETTA.)

O, Bird! How much better it would be
To let me die.

GREEN BIRD

Ninetta, stop your lament!
   try to be more grave,
For soon from this inhuman grave,
   from this misery you will be sent.

NINETTA

How's that? The Green Bird speaks!

GREEN BIRD

Be not surprised, Ninetta!
I am the son of a king, and in my first youth
Into the Green Bird by a wizard was changed,
In the hands of Barbarina, your daughter and my future mate,
Lies our good fortune, the release from our fate.

---

* A reference to *The Love of Three Oranges*. Ninetta was the daughter of King Concul,
  the third girl hidden in an orange by a witch.

Ninetta

O caro Augel, mi narra, e qual mia colpa
mi tien sepolta in quest'immonda stanza?
Ch'e del mio sposo, e de' miei cari figli?

Augello

L'odio di Tartagliona è la colpa tua sola.
T'ha accusata d'adultera a Tartaglia, figliola.
In cambio di due figli, scrisse al Re, tuo marito,
che un mufferle e una mufferla avevi partorito.
I figli non son morti;
L'uno si chiama Renzo, e l'altra Barbarina.
Se i tuoi gemelli vincono i perigli tremendi,
tu dall'immonda fossa l'usato trono ascendi;
perisce Tartagliona; io lascio queste spoglie,
se Barbarina è forte, e la prendo per moglie.
Ma, o dio, ch'io son forzato ad esserle avversario.
Ninetta, più non dico; ti volgo il taffanario.

(Dopo un'altra pantomima — più breve questa volta — l'Augellino esce di scena.)

Ninetta

Mente, resisti; chi le gran cose intese!
Prendiamo il cibo e preci al ciel si mandino.
Se dopo diciott'anni di sepolcro
trovo d'uscir la via,
storia non v'è, che superi la mia.

(Esce.)

NINETTA

O, dear Green Bird, do tell me what mistake
Of mine has kept me buried in this filthy hole?
What happened to my spouse and children dear?

GREEN BIRD

Your only guilt had been Queen Tartagliona's hate,
From her claim of adultery to Tartaglia comes your fate,
To him, the King, your husband, for your sins,
You gave birth to two puppies, not to twins,
And the twins are not dead.
Old Pantalone, that good-hearted Venetian did contrive
To see that your twins are still alive.
One's named Renzo and the other Barbarina. To them unknown,
Your destiny and mine is in their hands alone.
If terrible perils your twins overcome,
Tartagliona will perish, and, crowned, you'll ascend from
This filthy hole; I'll drop this disguise.
If Barbarina is strong, she'll recognize
Me, as Prince. Oh, God!, let my being her enemy pass,
Oh, Ninetta, no more may I say, as I leave, excuse my ass.

(Exits)

NINETTA

Oh, mind! Keep sane despite the shock of this news.
Let me eat this food and pray to stay alive.
If, after eighteen years of being buried,
I find an escape,
There will be no story stranger than mine.

(Exits)

45

Scena VII

(Entra Pantalone, che con la mano saluta l'esercito di Tartaglia che torna dalla guerra. Entrano i soldati con braccia e gambe fasciate, stampelle e una carriola che porta i resti di un combattente. Tartaglia è in testa. Dopo un giro l'esercito si schiera per le decorazioni. Piccolissime per i soldati e per l'asino. Smisurate e numerose per Tartaglia. Pantalone parla all'orecchio del re, che durante la seguente battuta manda tutti fuori a calci.)

Tartaglia

E piantatela con quei piffferi, non rompetemi la testa con suonate! Sono secco annoiato, scocciato, imbestialito, stanco! Non voglio vedere più nessuno!

Pantalone

(a parte)

Che Sua Maestà ha la luna. Vorrebbe congratularsi dei ribelli soggiogati del suo arrivo: ma ha sogezione, perchè di mal umore, e lo conosce un re strambo, come un cavallo.

Tartaglia

Questo è il pavimento dove passeggiava la mia Ninetta. Di là lo spazzacucina, dove il quondam Re, padre della mia Ninetta, la fece ritirare il giorno del solenne sfortunato imeneo. Oh giorni felici, ore di dolci tenerezze, notti d'amore accanto alla mia Ninetta.

SCENE VII

(In front of the Royal Palace. Military music. Pantomime of the soldiers returning from the war, TARTAGLIA is at the head of the army, which is composed of six mimes. They have legs in plaster, missing arms, broken trumpets. One without a head is pushed in on a pushcart. Military parade.)

TARTAGALIA

(Where underlined; he stutters.)

Stop those trumpets!

(Fifes and pipes.)

Don't break my head with that fanfare! I'm bored stiff, annoyed, ready to fly into a passion, tired. I don't want to see anyone, anymore.

(Soldiers exit.)

PANTALONE
(Enters)
(Aside)

It seems to me that his Majesty has gone a bit out of his mind. I'd like to congratulate him on putting down the rebels, but he is as unstrung as a lame horse.

TARTAGLIA

This is the very pavement where my Ninetta used to walk. There is the gallery where the King, father of Ninetta, had her presented to me on that solemn and ill-fated day of our wedding. Days of happiness! O, sweet hours of tenderness! Nights of love! Near my Ninetta.

(Pause.)

TARTAGLIA

Get out! At once, or I'll leave you locked up.

Pantalone

(a parte)

Che gli sembra, che Sua Maestà pianga; che giurerebbe, che piange
la povera regina sposa, da diciott'anni seppellita sotto il buco della
scaffa.

Tartaglia

Che non sarà piu felice senza Ninetta.

Pantalone

Maestà, perméssó . . .

Tartaglia

Che Volete?!!

Pantalone

Perdonami, si da coraggio, si fa innanzi: sua congratulazione de
ribelli soggiogati; suoi di felicità. Parergli, che sia malinconico; che
gli vede gli occhi rossi. Chi gli sembra, che Sua Maestà pianga?

Tartaglia

Chi sia, che pianga? Qual coraggio si prenda?

Pantalone

Sua Maestà, non sia di mal umore. Il suo melanconico mi fa abbat-
tuto.

Tartaglia

Che parlare sia quello? Non voler che i ministri si prendano tal
confidenza con un re, suo pari. Parta subito; altrimenti lo farà porre
in berlina. Parta!

PANTALONE

(Aside.)

I have the impression his Majesty is crying about his poor Queen Ninetta, who has been buried for eighteen years under the toilets, Your Majesty . . .

TARTAGLIA

I'll never be happy without you, Ninetta.

PANTALONE

Majesty, allow me . . .

TARTAGLIA

What do you want?!!

PANTALONE

Forgive me, if I am too forward; I would like to congratulate his Majesty for his victory against the rebels. These are good signs for happiness. His Majesty seems a little pale, and his eyes are red. Has his Majesty been crying?

TARTAGLIA

Who is crying? How dare you say that your King has been crying!

PANTALONE

Don't get mad, your Majesty. I said it because it pains me to see you so woebegone.

TARTAGLIA

What kind of talk is this? I do not let my ministers take such liberties with their King. Get out! At once, or I'll have you locked up. Out of here!

Pantalone

Che aveva brama di introdursi, e di dirgli qualche cosa, e la stramberia del Monarca, vuol che gli sia tagliata la lingua, se parla. Chi ha il cane per la coda, si sbrighi.

(Esce)

Tartaglia

Oh, misera sorte di noi poveri monarchi; dover piangere di nascosto, non poter dar sfogo al dolore, dover serrare nel petto i singulti, sorridere quando l'animo è colmo di disperazione, acciochè i ministri non iscoprano la nostra debolezza e i sudditi ci rispettino! Oh, non aver alcun amico a cui confidare la mia doglia interna! Sapevo di avere un amico intrinseco, un confidente in Truffaldino cuoco, ma, ahimè, mi sono ingannato. Il perfido dopo aver guadagnato dei soldi a Corte, divenne superbo, s'ammogliò con Smeraldina, e aperta bottega da salsicciaio, ebbe cuore di abbandonarmi. Ma ora che sono solo posso lasciare la gravità regale e finalmente sfogare il mio dolore e far delle pazzie a mio modo.

(Tartaglia prorompe in ragli asineschi.)

Scena VIII

(Entra Truffaldino.)

PANTALONE
(Aside)

I wanted to warn him of what has happened at the palace, but he wants to cut out my tongue before I say anything. Who has a dog by the tail, had better run fast!

(Exit PANTALONE.)

TARTAGLIA

(Pause.)

O, miserable destiny of us poor Kings! To have to hide our tears; we can't give vent to our sorrow. We must keep back our sighs, we must smile when full of despair; so that our ministers do not discover our weaknesses; that our subjects respect us. Ah, not have one single friend to whom to confide the deep pain in my heart. I once thought I had a friend in the palace, the cook Truffaldino, but I was mistaken in him. That false friend made a little money at court and turned into a snob. He married Smeraldina, opened a sausage shop, and had the heart to leave me.

(Pause.)

But now that I'm alone at last, I can throw off Royal dignity and give vent to my grief. Do the crazy things I want to do.

(He dances, brays, rolls on the floor like a baby trying to suck his toes.)

SCENE VIII

(Enter TRUFFALDINO.)

Truffaldino

(Sangue de mi! L'ho dito mi che l'è Tartaja! M'ha bastà vegnir drio a la real vose!) Maestà . . .

Tartaglia

(Truffaldino! Quale vergogna! Egli mi ha udito piangere). Che vuoi Truffaldino?

Truffaldino

Ho abuo gnove de lu e, in nome de la vechia amicizia, non m'ho poduo tegnir de congratularme e de renovarghe la memoria del me amor; s'arecordelo quando ghe gratava la schena co i pironi da cosena? e ghe cavava i peoci da la crena?

Tartaglia

Come stai?

Truffaldino

Ben. Le orine l'è chiare: ho una gran fame lupa sempre compagna note e dì, avanti de magnà e dopo magnà; evacuo ogni zorno all'istessa ora, con soddisfazion per servirla . . .

Tartaglia

Ami sempre Smeraldina?

TRUFFALDINO

(Aside.)

I'll be damned! I'd swear that that's Tartaglia! I think I recognize the royal voice.
Your Majesty!

(Pause.)

TARTAGLIA

(Aside.)

Truffaldino! How embarrassing! He has heard me crying. What, Truffaldino, do you want?

TRUFFALDINO

I have heard that you were back and in the name of our old friendship, I rushed to congratulate you and to remind you of my long devotion, Do you remember when I used to scratch your back with a poker and I picked the lice from your head?

TARTAGLIA

So how are you, friend Truffaldino?

TRUFFALDINO

Fine. My piss is still crystal clear. I stay as hungry as a wolf, both night and day: before I eat dinner and after I eat. At the same hour every day, I have a good shit! My pleasure! At your service!

TARTAGLIA

You still love Smeraldina?

Truffaldino

La tasa, Maestà! Ghe gh'ho volù ben i primi quindeze dì, ma po' l'ha principià a farme schifo. Parlo col cuor in man.

> (Mette la mano sul deretano, dove accanto alle altre toppe, è dipinto un grande cuore rosso. Così farà ogni volta che dirà questa battuta.)

Truffaldino

Dopo i primi tatarezzi, l'amor l'è andà in t'i calcagni; l'ha un caratterin che non se pol andar d'accordo; no l'è gnente filosofa. Parlo col cuor in man.

Tartaglia

Come sarebbe a dire, Truffaldino?

Truffaldino

Parlo col cuor in man. L'è una dona all'antica. Figurarse, la se tol de le rogne per dei bastardi; figurarse, la sleva orfani; figurarse, la se cava el pan dala bocca per darlo ai poareti; figurarse, piena dei pregiudizi, de sciempiae, de debolezze che fa vegnir el late ai zenoci. Parlo col cuor in man.

Tartaglia

Solo per questo t'è venuta a noia o anche per altre cagioni?

Truffaldino

Parlo col cuor in man. A zonta de ste stolidesse, de zorno in zorno, le so belesse l'è deventae oridesse, a punto tal che, per refarme la boca, me tocca revisitar certe casete a pian terren. Parlo col cuor in man.

TRUFFALDINO

O, don't mention *her* name, your Majesty! I loved her for the first two weeks. After that she started to disgust me. I am speaking with my heart in hand.

> (He places his hand on the seat of his pants where there's a big red heart.)

After the first skirmishes, love went down to my heels. With her disposition it's impossible to get along with her. She's not a philosopher. I am speaking with my heart in hand.

> (Business, as above.)

TARTAGLIA

How can you say that, Truffaldino!

TRUFFALDINO

With my heart in hand: she's old fashioned! Imagine she took in two bastards, think of it! She raised them; two orphans; just think of it, she took the bread out of my mouth to give it to the little wretches. Just think of it, she is so sentimental, stupid, spineless, that she makes me weak in the knees. I am speaking with my heart in hand!

TARTAGLIA

Is that the only reason you're bored with her? Are there other reasons?

TRUFFALDINO

I am speaking with my heart in hand. Besides all that nonsense, from day to day, what was once her beauty changed to horror, and to such a point, that to lift my spirits, I had to visit certain houses at their ground-floor prices. I am speaking with my heart in hand. After

Truffaldino

Dopo disdot'anni de matrimonio l'è tanta bruta che la me fa pì schifo de la cassia e de l'ojo de riceno. Parlo col cuor in man.

Tartaglia

(Comincio a scoprire che Truffaldino non viene a me in buona amicizia) Dimmi un po': come vanno gli affari?

Truffaldino

Parlo col cuor in man. So' falìo marzo, Maestà, ma non per colpa mia. Quella mata de Smeraldina, l'ha una testa che no la magna gnanca i porsei; l'ha fatto credenza, limosine e alter afar rovinosi . . .

Tartaglia

E tu denari, non ne hai sprecati?

Truffaldino

L'è vero che son stà a l'ostaria, ma rare volte; solo do volte al zorno, per coltivar amici a sentir qualche bona massima filosofica.

Tartaglia

E non hai frequentato qualche donna?

Truffladino

Parlo col cuor in man. Solo per sollevarme de l'antipatia de quella striga de Smeraldina. Per alter per far economia ho cercà semper done senza naso, orbe de un ocio, gobe, con qualche piaga in te le gambe, carghe de rogna francesina che le puzzasse, con sopportazion, come un cadavere. . .

eighteen years of marriage, she became so ugly she was like taking castor oil, I couldn't look her in the eye. I am speaking with my heart in hand.

TARTAGLIA

(Aside.)

I suspect that Truffaldino has not come to me in true friendship. Pray tell me, how's business?

TRUFFALDINO

I am speaking with my heart in hand. I am stone broke, your Majesty, but through no fault of mine. That crazy Smeraldina has a head no pig would eat! She's always giving credit, money, everything to ruin me.

TARTAGLIA

And your money? Did you not squander it away?

TRUFFALDINO

It's true I went to taverns, but very, very seldom! No more than twice a day! . . . so I could make some friends, and learn a philosophical maxim, or two.

TARTAGLIA

And did you not frequent certain women?

TRUFFALDINO

I am speaking with my heart in hand. Only to find solace for the outrages of that witch, Smeraldina. To save a bit of money, I sought out those ladies without noses, cockeyed, hunchbacked, with sores on their legs, or infected with the French disease that makes them smell so bad they're almost like a corpse.

Tartaglia

(Truffaldino non è altro che un becco cornuto di prima sfera, un filosofo moderno da guardarsi! Non sono persuaso che venga per buona amicizia, ma per il bisogno in cui si trova). Ascoltami Truffaldino, dimmi la verità; se tu non avessi l'appetito che ti tormentasse, se tu amassi ancora Smeraldina, se i negozi della bottega andassero ancora floridamente, saresti venuto in traccia di me per rinnovare l'amicizia? Rispondi il vero, altrimenti ti farò cavar le budelle e il cuore.

Truffaldino

El me lassa pensarghe un pochetto.

Tartaglia

Spicciati a dir il vero o ti faccio tagliare a pezzi.

Truffaldino

Parlo col cuor in man. Se non avessi sta fame orba, se avesse ancora boresso per quel cancaro de dona, se vendesse ancora panzete e straculi, Re e Monarchi me passarae pel cervelo co fa le strasse da pìe in te la boca.

Tartaglia

(Durante queste battute, manda fuori a calci Truffaldino. Quindi si abbandona a ragli di disperazione.)

Fuori di qui, sciaguarto canaglia. Fuori, prima ch'io ti faccia squartare.

Truffaldino

Ajiuto, ajiuto. El xe mato, fermelo, leghelo, chè el xe deventà mato.

(Esce.)

TARTAGLIA

(Aside.)

Truffaldino is a number one cuckold, and as for being a modern philosopher, I'll beware of him! I don't think it is friendship that prompted him to come here, but to see whatever he can get from me. Listen to me, Truffaldino, tell the truth; if hunger didn't torment you, if you were still in love with Smeraldina, if your shop were still doing good business, would you have come to me to try to renew our friendship? Tell me the truth, or, I will have your guts and heart torn out.

TRUFFALDINO

Just let me think a little bit.

TARTAGLIA

Quick! Tell me the truth or I'll have you cut in pieces.

TRUFFALDINO

I am speaking with my heart in hand. If I did not have this hunger that has made me blind, if I still were interested in that eyesore Smeraldina, if my shop still sold sausages and bacon, I can assure you that no thought of kings or monarchs would get into my brain.

TARTAGLIA

Get out of here, you rogue! You knave! Get out of here before I have you hanged and quartered.

TRUFFALDINO

Help! Help! The King has lost his mind! Stop him! Tie him up! He's gone crazy!

(He runs out.)

Tartaglia

Si, pazzo, pazzo dal dolore, dalla disperazione. Ninetta! Ninetta!

(Colpi di tosse catarrosa di Tartagliona.)

Ma ecco la regina,

(Altri colpi di tosse.)

mia madre.

Scena IX

(Apre le braccia, ma il figlio, indignato, le volta le spalle. Tartagliona sempre con le braccia protese per un abbraccio — durante la seguente battuta — si avvicina a Tartaglia.)

Tartagliona

Figlio, così mi tratti? Ove si vide
che dopo diciott'anni che sta lunge
dal sen materno un figlio, giunto al fine
si perda per la corte in bagatelle,

(Tartagliona è giunta vicino al figlio, fa per abbracciarlo, Tartaglia si scosta e la vecchia per poco non finisce per terra.)

pria di correre ansante, a dare un bacio
sulla destra real della sua madre?

Tartaglia

Signora madre cara, vi scongiuro,

TARTAGLIA

Yes, I'm mad! I'm mad from sorrow, and from desperation! Ninetta, Ninetta!

(Coughing of the Queen Mother.)

TARTAGLIA

But here is the Queen,

(More coughs.)

my Mother!

SCENE IX

TARTAGLIONA

(Opening her arms, but her son, indignant turns his back on her. TARTAGLIONA, still with her arms open, begs for an embrace, as she approaches TARTAGLIA.)

Is this the way you treat me, son?
For eighteen years, no less!
Torn from a mother's breast
Now that the court for you is won, you waste your time in foolishness.

(TARTAGLIONA lunges to embrace her son. TARTAGALIA steps aside, and old TARTAGLIONA nearly falls to the ground.)

And do not run to place a kiss
Upon your royal mother's hand?

TARTAGLIA

Madame, dear mother, I do beg of you

Tartaglia

a ritirarvi nelle vostre stanze,
e a lasciar in pace un disperato.

Tartagliona

O temerario figlio; io già ti leggo
nel profondo del cor. Di Tartagliona
figlio non sembri. Io so che ti rincresce
di Ninetta la morte, e che più care
avevi le tue corna, di tua madre.
Sovvengati chi son, da chi discendo,
che la regina de' Tarocchi io sono.

Tartaglia

Signora madre, una vecchia decrepita
qual siete voi, doveva usar prudenza,
io sono un giovanetto poco esperto
ed il sangue mi bolle.
So che odiavate quella poveretta . . .
Non vi dico di più . . . Signora madre,
vi prego a ritirarvi e non seccate
d'un Re sdegnato le figliali natiche.

Tartagliona

Vecchia a me? Sommi Dei che ingiuria è questa!
Ingrato! Cosi parli a chi nel ventre
ti portò pel girar di nove lune?

Tartaglia

Pagherò un asinello, che vi porti
per quante lune san girare in cielo.

(TARTAGLIA)

Return now to your quarters
Leave a desperate man in peace.

TARTAGLIONA

Oh, audacious son! As I look now
Deep into your heart, you do not seem
To be Tartagliona's son.
How well I know you mourn
The death of your Ninetta and you'd rather
Be a cuckold than your mother's little boy.
Remember who I am, who my forebears are, I am the Queen of
     the Tarot.

TARTAGLIA

Madame, mother, an old decrepit woman
Like yourself had best take care.
I am your little boy
Whose blood's about to boil!
I know how much you hated that poor girl . . .
I will not say another word . . . Madame, my mother.
I advise you to get out and not to vex
The buttocks of a king distraught!

TARTAGLIONA

Decrepit's what you call me? God in heaven! Such an insult!
Ungrateful child! Is this the way to speak to one
Who for nine moons once held you in her womb?

TARTAGLIA

I'll gladly pay a donkey to hold you
For as many moons as travel in the sky!

Tartagliona

Figlio disumano! Ti ricorda,
ingratissimo figlio, che, bambino,
non volli balie, e che i miei propri petti
ti diero il latte, ch'or così mi paghi.

Tartaglia

Quando passan le femmine dal latte,
io ve ne pagherò venti mastelle.
Così posso pagar il benefizio;
ma voi non mi potete render viva
la mia Ninetta, di Concul figliola.
Un povero monarca, affaticato
in guerra diciott'anni, giunge al trono,
crede di riposar nel caro seno
della consorte, e trova ch'ella è morta,
sepolta sotto il buco della scafa.
Non ho più moglie, amici più non trovo;
per me non v'è più pace in questo mondo.

(Si appoggia — ragliando disperato — sulla spalla della
madre. Durante la battuta seguente la Tartagliona, con grot-
tesco amore materno, lo diverte con giochi infantili. Tartaglia
ride, batte le mani.)

Tartagliona

Figlio, ti vo' scusar, ma da viltade
troppo sei preso. Il tuo dolor solleva.
Giocheremo ogni giorno a gatta cieca,
e tocca ferro, a romper la pignatta . . .

TARTAGLIONA

Inhuman son! Remember this,
Ungrateful child, when you were just a baby,
And not yet to nurses given,
I it was who suckled you upon my breasts, and this is how you
     repay me.

TARTAGLIA

When the milkmaids come around,
I'll pay for twenty vats for you.
That's how I'll see that you're repaid.
But you, you never can give back her life
To my Ninetta, of King Concul the daughter.
Poor monarch that I am, exhausted
By these eighteen years of war, returning to the throne,
Thinking I could rest my head on the breast
Of my dear wife, and find her dead,
Buried underneath the toilets,
I have no wife, I have no friends.
For me, in all this world, there is no peace.

     (Leans — while braying desperately — on his mother.)

     (During the following speech, TARTAGLIONA diverts him
     with childish tricks. TARTAGLIA laughs and claps his hands.)

TARTAGLIONA

Son, I forgive you, but you are too faint-hearted.
Your sorrow will grow lighter.
Each day we shall play hide and seek,
And hopscotch, and some blind man's bluff . . .

Tartaglia

(D'improvviso interrompe il gioco e si adira.)

Signora madre, burla troppo grande
fu il seppellir la mia Ninetta viva.
Giungano pur le Ninfe della Bragola,
tutte le Dee della Calle de' Corli;
insensibil sarò. Mi fate rabbia;
vi prego, andate via.

Tartagliona

Rabbia la madre!
Scacciar la madre! O ciel, lo fulminate.

(La vecchia tossisce con molto catarro. Durante la battuta
seguente di Tartaglia — alla fine di ogni proposizione — si
inserisce con altri colpi di tosse, sempre di natura ritmico-
musicale.)

Tartaglia

Voi non volete andar; dove voi siete
non ho flemma di star. Vedo che in seno
vi si muove il catarro. Il mio rispetto
vuol ch'io vi lasci, e me ne vada a letto.

(Esce dalla scena, adiratissimo. La vecchia continua a tossire.)

Tartagliona

Oimè, la rabbia . . . Oimè, il catarro in moto
M'opprime la trachea . . . Sento ch'io crepo.
Ecco il castigo che mi manda il cielo.

(Smette improvvisamente di tossire.)

O strologo, o poeta, a tempo giugni.

TARTAGLIA

(Suddenly stopping the game.)

Madame, my mother, it was too great a jest
To bury my Ninetta, while she lived.
Gather nymphs in from the woods,
The goddesses from Olympus Hill;
I'd be indifferent to them. You drive me mad;
I beg of you to go away!

TARTAGLIONA

Your mother drives you mad!
Your mother you would chase away? Oh, heavens, hit him with a
    thunderbolt!

(She coughs with much catarrh. During TARTAGLIA's
speech, until the end of each sentence, TARTAGLIONA inter-
jects coughs, always musical and rhythmical.)

TARTAGLIA

You will not go? To hold the two of us,
No spot is big enough. I have no desire to stay,
I see that you are choking. Respect for myself
Bids me leave you. I'm going off to bed.

TARTAGLIONA

Ah, my anger! Ah! Rage is choking me!
I feel I'm just about to croak.
This is the punishment that heaven sends me.

(Suddenly she stops coughing.)

Oh, Astrologer! Oh, Poet! You have come here just in time.

Scena X

Brighella

(Guarda verso l'alto e mima le battute che recita. Di tanto in tanto si avvicina alla vecchia, guardandola con finta passione.)

Fiamme voraci
che rischiarate
questa mia mente,
ne m'abbruciaste,
io stava meglio
nell'ignoranza.
Ahi, Tartagliona,
che val costanza?

Tartagliona

Che mi vuoi dir, poeta? Io non t'intendo.

Brighella

Sono vicini i Gemini,
già le mura s'innalzano;
questa è notte terribile,
tu puoi trarti le cottole,
e dalle pulci scuoterle,
che l'ora è di dormir.
Io veglierò qual nottola,
e ti trarrò la cabala;
tutto farò il possibile
dal destin per difenderti;
ma il capo lavo all'asino,
ma temo di fallir.

Tartagliona

Oh, maledetto strologo!

SCENE X

BRIGHELLA

(Gazing into his crystal ball.)

Oh flames voracious
That illuminate
My mind;
You burn me.
I was better
In ignorance.
Ah, Tartagliona,
What is the worth of constancy?

TARTAGLIONA

What do you mean to tell me, Poet? I don't understand you.

BRIGHELLA

The Twins are near;
Already walls are rising;
This is to be a terrible night;
You'd best take off your petticoats,
And shake from them the fleas.
The time has now come to sleep.
Like a bat I'll watch you, and I will peruse your horoscope.
All that's possible I'll do,
From destiny I shall protect you;
I lose both time and effort*
While fearing that I'll only fail.

TARTAGLIONA

(Aside.)

O, cursed Astrologer!

---

*Gozzi, Carlo, *Opere, Teatro e Polemiche Teatrali*, Editor, Petronio Giuseppe, Milano. Publisher Rizzoli editore, 1962. The idiom: *Ma il capo lavo all'asino* is the idiom 'But I wash the head of an ass' translates as 'I'm losing time and effort.'

Tartagliona

Io non intendo un diavolo.
Alle minacce orribili
le natiche mi tremano,
nè so cosa pensar.

Brighella

(Rivolto in direzione del pubblico, descrive con le mani una
sfera, nella quale guarda fissamente.)

Care pupille amabili. . .
Ah, troppo dissi; scusami.
Occhio che sempre lagrima. . .
ah, maestà, perdonami.
Possenti baranbagole,
per voi son temerario. . .
Ma ohimè, ch'io veggo nella terza sfera
il mio tesoro, biscia scodellera!

(TARTAGLIONA)

I don't understand one damned thing.
At your terrible predictions.
What tremors shake my poor behind!
I don't know what to think.

BRIGHELLA

(Describing with his hands a sphere, in which he looks fixedly.)

Ah, lovable apple of my eye . . .
Oh, I'm saying too much; excuse me.

(Forgetting himself.)

Ugh, your red-moist eyes . . .

(Catching himself.)

Ah, Majesty, forgive me.
You have such gross and flabby breasts*

(Having forgotten himself.)

For you am I daring . . .
But, oh alas, I see in the third sphere,
Oh, my treasure, a turtle appears!

---

* The Venetian word, *barambagole,* translates idomatically as gross and flabby breasts of an old woman.

**Gozzi, opere, p. 179

(La Tartagliona gli si avvicina e cerca di scrutare nella sfera; non riesce a vedere nulla; vi soffia l'alito e quindi la pulisce con la mano e con la manica. Durante questa scena mimica, Brighella confida al pubblico la seguente battuta:)

Brighella

L'estro m'ha servì pulito.
Spero de aver fatto qualche colpo. Se potesse ridurla a far un testamento in mio favor, non saria scontento delle mie amorose attenzioni, e del frutto dei miei poetici sudori.

(Esce di scena, ripetendo la battuta "Care pupille amibili . . ."
La vecchia lo segue, incantata, e si ferma all'uscita.)

Tartagliona

Gli oscuri sensi di costui mi mettono
in grave agitazion. La tenerezza
ch'ei dimostra per me, sperar mi lascia.
S'eseguisca il consiglio, abbian riposo
le membra idolatrate del più insigne
poeta ch'abbia il secolo. Non mancano
in me vezzi, e lusinghe, ond'al mio fianco
fedel sia sempre. Ah, non vorrei, che alfine
le mie finezze a lui negli altri amanti
destasser gelosia. Stelle infelici!
Sino i meriti miei mi son nimici.

(La vecchia esce di scena, alternando esclamazioni di gioia e di vezzo a violenti scoppi di tosse.)

(TARTAGLIONA draws near him and tries to look into the sphere; not able to see anything, she breathes heavily and wrings her hands. During this scene of miming, BRIGHELLA confides to the audience the following speech.)

BRIGHELLA

(To audience.)

My intuition served me right
I hope that I've impressed her
To make out her will in my favor.
She'd not be displeased with my amorous attentions with the fruit of
    my poet's sweat.

(Exits.)

TARTAGLIONA

The obscure words of this man cause me
Great anxiety. The affection
That he shows me gives me hope.
I had better follow his suggestion and rest this body,
So adored by the greatest
Poet of our century. I'm not lacking
Charm or enticements, and at my side
He'll be faithful forever. I hope that
For my other lovers
My favors to him will not arouse jealousy. Unhappy stars!
Even my beauty is my enemy.

(The old QUEEN TARTAGLIONA is about to exit, alternating between exclamations of joy and violent coughs.)

Scena XI

(La reggia di Tartaglia si sposta sulla destra in avanti. Al lato
sinistro entra una delle case della scena I, da dietro della quale
appaiono silenziosamente, avvolti in ampi mantelli, Renzo e
Barbarina, che vengono a porsi a destra, proprio sotto la
reggia.)

Barbarina

Renzo, questa è la reggia, e questo è il sasso,
che Calmon statua ci additò. Che pensi
che nasca nel scagliarlo?

Renzo

Ei ci promise
che allo scagliar del sasso sarem ricchi.
Scaglialo, non tardar.

Barbarina

Tu dunque
brami diventar ricco. A poco a poco
perdi filosofia.

Renzo

Senti sorella;
non mi dir mai così. Questo rimprovero
mi fa quasi scordar la fame e il freddo;
amo filosofia, nè mi vergogno
di quella passion nobil, ch'ho in seno

Barbarina

Renzo, io non scaglio il sasso.

SCENE XI

(TARTAGLIA's Palace moves on from the right. Left is the 'house' wing from Scene I. From the right enter silently the twins, wrapped in ample mantles. RENZO and BARBARINA come almost up to the Palace.)

BARBARINA

Renzo, this is the Palace, and this is the stone
That Calmon told us to pick up. What do you think
Will happen if we throw it?

RENZO

He said
If we throw the stone we'll be rich.
Throw it. Don't hesitate.

BARBARINA

So you
Want to be rich. Little by little
You're losing your philosophical detachment.

RENZO

Listen, sister,
Don't keep telling me that. Your chiding
Almost makes me forget hunger and cold;
I love philosophy, and I am not ashamed
Of this noble passion I have in my heart.

BARBARINA

Renzo, I'll not throw the stone.

Renzo

Si, sì, lo scaglia;
Non dubitar. Nelle ricchezze ancora
filosofi saremo.

Barbarina

La fame e il freddo ragionar ti fanno?
Ah, Renzo, io temo assai ch'ogni filosofo
sia mosso a ragionar da fame e freddo.

Renzo

Scaglialo, scaglialo!

Barbarina

Il sasso io scaglio,
e voglia il ciel ch'io non mi scordi mai,
che un vilissimo sasso non curato
delle ricchezze mie sia la sorgente.

(Scaglia il sasso. Tuoni, lampi, terremoto. Atmosfera apocalittica. I due cadono per terra, tramortiti.
Alla sinistra la piccola casa scompare e lascia posto ad un magnifico palazzo, che sfolgora di luce. Ai lati due servi negri con grandi candelabri. Renzo e Barbarina si alzano, lasciando i mantelli, si avvicinano al palazzo e si accorgono che i loro miseri abiti si sono mutati in vestiti ricchissimi, tempestati di pietre preziose.)

Renzo

Sorella! Ah, che mai veggio! Io son confuso.

RENZO

Yes, yes, throw it!
Trust me. We can be rich
And still be philosophers.

BARBARINA

Do hunger and cold make you act this way?
I fear many a philosopher
Thinks this way from hunger and cold.

RENZO

Throw it, throw it!

BARBARINA

I throw the stone,
And I hope by heaven that I will never forget
That a mean and indifferent stone
Was the source of my riches.

> (She throws the stone. Thunder and lightning. The twins fall to
> the ground. At the left the little 'house' wing moves off and in
> its place moves on a 'palace' wing. Enter from each side of the
> palace two black servants with large candelabra. RENZO and
> BARBARINA rise, casting off their mantles. As they approach
> the palace they realize that their miserable clothes have been
> changed into rich robes, adorned with precious stones.)

RENZO

Sister! What do I see! I am confused.

Barbarina

Diamo or fede a Calmon. Questo palagio,
non ci lusinghi di felicitade,
ch'ei ci predisse ancor pianti e sventure.

(Entrano nel palazzo.)

Scena XII

BRIGHELLA E TARTAGLIONA

Brighella

(Esce portando con due mani la balaustra del verone. L'appoggia. Guardia incantato il palazzo dei Gemelli e con il gesto
chiama Tartagliona.)

Fronte crespa, u'mirando io mi scoloro,
dove spunta i suoi strali amore e morte.

Tartagliona

Deh, poeta, mi di' questo palagio
che si risplende in maestosa mole,
e di ricchezza questa reggia avanza,
come mai nacque in una sola notte?

Brighella

Regina, del mio cor parte più cara,
io tutto so, ma dirtelo non posso.
Solo dirò che del palagio altero
gli abitatori a rovinar son giunti
quelle labbra di latte, quelle ciglia,
rare, di bianca neve, e i quondam petti.

Tartagliona

Ah, lascia, lascia il favellar oscuro;

BARBARINA

Now let us heed what Calmon said. This palace!
Don't let it delude us;
Calmon predicted that there would still be tears and misfortunes.

(They enter the Palace.)

SCENE XII

BRIGHELLA

(Entering carrying two palace balustrades; he places each. He looks, amazed, at the palace of the twins, and with a gesture he brings on TARTAGLIONA.)

Wrinkled forehead, whence shoot arrows
Of love and death! Beholding you I grow pale.

TARTAGLIONA

Ah, Poet, tell me! The place that I see before me:
So resplendent and majestic
Of a size and beauty that surpasses my own.
How could it have been created in one single night?

BRIGHELLA

Queen, dearest part of my heart.
I know everything, but I cannot tell you.
I will only say that the inhabitants of this lofty palace
Are joined together to ruin:
These lips of milk, these extraordinary eyebrows,
And, these unusual breasts of white snow.

TARTAGLIONA

Ah, stop, stop this obscure talk!

Tartagliona

Tutto spera da me; ma de' m'addita.
come rovinar possa chi procura
di rovinarmi; in te solo confido.

Brighella

Maestà, delizia del mio estro poetico, prima de tutto e per tutto
quanto che pol nascer, la consegio a far el so testamento, e a no
desmentegarse de beneficar chi ghe vol ben, e che pol immortalar el
so nome con un poema superior al rugginoso dente del tempo e alle
critiche, figlie della calliginosa invidia.

Tartagliona

Deh, non mi funestar; sono ancor fresca,
pensa a salvarmi e a celebrarmi in vita.

Brighella

(A parte.)

(l'e dura in sul testamento, 'sta befana) Ghe parlo fura dei denti, con
verità contraria all'istinto poetico; xe difficile el poderla salvar dalle
rovine, che ghe sta sora la testa. Tuttavia la me ascolta ben. I abitatori
del quel palazzo xe un zovenetto e una zovenetta, fradello e sorella, i
quali, prima de diventar ricchi, gera do pitocchi, filosofi per la vita;
adesso che in t'una notta i xe diventai ricchi a martelletto, i ha perso
la tramontana della folosofia, e i gh'ha in testa tutta la vanità del
mondo. No i pol soffrir che ghe sia rimproverà niente, che ghe manca
niente, de no superar tutti in tutto. Per sta strada se deve tentar la so
distruzion.

(TARTAGLIONA)

All that you want from me you can have:
If you will tell me how to destroy these two who've come here
To ruin me. I have faith only in you.

BRIGHELLA

Majesty, light of my poetic spirit, first of all and for all who are to be born: make a will for the benefit of one who loves you intensely, who is thinking of immortalizing your name in a poem that will outlast the rusty teeth of time and all critics, those descendants of dark envy!

TARTAGLIONA

Don't depress me! I'm still young.
Think of preserving me, glorifying me in life.

BRIGHELLA

(Aside.)

She is really tough about the will, the old hag! I'll speak frankly, tell her the truth — which is contrary to my poetic inspiration.

(To TARTAGLIONA.)

It is very difficult to save you from ruination. It hangs over your head. But listen carefully to me. The inhabitants of that palace are a boy and a girl — brother and sister, who before becoming rich, were two hopelessly poor philosophers. Now, in a night, they became rich and lost sight of philosophy. Their heads are full of all the vanities of the world. They can't stand criticism. They lack nothing. They think they are superior in everything. Along these lines we will attempt their destruction.

Tartagliona

Dimmi più oltre: io ben saprò ubbidirti.

Brighella

Maestà, fatal al mio cuor, ella sa quanto mortal sia l'impresa dell'acquisto del pomo che canta, della acqua d'oro che suona e balla e dell'Augel Belverde, oggetti poco fora della città, posseduti dalla Fata Serpentina.

Tartagliona

So che funesto è il luogo; e che per questo?

Brighella

Bisogna donca che la procura de veder la zovenetta, che abita in quel palazzo, la qual za ha perso la traccia della filosofia, e xe deventada el tipo della vanità; e basterà schizzarghe in tel stomego, ste quattro parole tremende. La me ascolta ben:

(La battuta seguente viene scandita frase per frase dalla vecchia. Così avverrà anche per le altre due invettive, ma con ritmo sempre più rapido.)

"Voi siete belle assai; ma più bella sareste, s'un dei pomi che cantano in una mano avreste."

Tartagliona

Voi siete bella . . . ecc.

(Ripete la frase da sola, rivolgendosi al palazzo dei Gemelli.)

TARTAGLIONA

Tell me more. I will do what you say.

BRIGHELLA

Majesty, fatal to my heart, you know how dangerous it is to get the apple that sings, the golden water that dances and sings, and the Green Bird, all of which beyond the city, are in the possession of the Serpentine Fairy.

TARTAGLIONA

I know that the place is very dangerous. And what does that matter to me?

BRIGHELLA

You must meet the girl who lives in the palace. She has lost all her good sense and has become the image of vanity. Just tell her these few terrifying words: Listen well to me:

> (The following sentence in quotation is repeated phrase by phrase by TARTAGLIONA. She does it with a rhythm which becomes ever more rapid.)

"You are quite beautiful, but more beautiful you would be if in your hand you were to hold the apple that sings."

TARTAGLIONA

"You are quite beautiful, but more beautiful you would be if in your hand you were to hold the apple that sings."

> (Repeating the phrase, she leans over in the direction of the palace of the twins.)

Brighella

Bravissima! E dopo sbararghe st'altra bisinella: "Figlia, voi siete bella; ma più bella sareste s'acqua che suona e balla nell'altra mano aveste."

. Tartagliona

Figlia, voi siete bella. . .ecc.

Brighella

E po' ancora: "Figlia, voi siete bella assai, ma più bella sareste se in possesso l'Augel Belverde aveste"

Tartagliona

Figlia, voi siete . . . ecc.

Brighella

Soavissimamente! Da'ste parole la vedarà un effetto mirabile. Bisogna conosser el cuore uman nelle varie circostanze. Con 'ste parole i abitatori de quel palazzo xe rovinai, e se queste no basterà, gh'ho un altro colpo sicuro.

Tartagliona

Voi siete belle assai . . . ecc.

(Ripete tutte le frasi, inserendosi nelle pause della seguente battuta di Brighella e poi esce.)

BRIGHELLA

Excellent! Afterwards you pay her another compliment: "Daughter, you are beautiful, but even more beautiful you would be if in the other hand you were to hold a cup of the water that dances and sings."

TARTAGLIONA

"Daughter, you are beautiful, but even more beautiful you would be if in the other hand you were to hold a cup of the water that dances and sings."

BRIGHELLA

And then again, "Daughter, you are very beautiful, but even more beautiful you would be if you were to possess the Green Bird."

TARTAGLIONA

"Daughter, you are very beautiful, but even more beautiful you would be if you were to possess the Green Bird."

BRIGHELLA

Most sweetly! You'll see the miraculous results of these words. It's necessary to know human nature in all circumstances. With these words will be destroyed the inhabitants of that palace, and if that is not enough I have another way that will be certain.

TARTAGLIONA

"You are very beautiful . . . etc."

(She repeats all the phrases inserting them in the pauses of the following speech of BRIGHELLA and then exits.)

Brighella

Se faza tutto quel che xe pol per prolongar la vita a sta graziosa
antigaia. Ma se no la redugo a far testamento con un item favorevole,
cosa me giova l'apollinea fronda, la direzion profonda, la fiamma
che m'inonda? Lasso! Non di diamante, ma di vetro, veggio di man
cadermi ogni speranza.

(Esce, portando con sè la balaustra del verone.)

SCENA XIII

(Esce dalla scena la reggia di Tartaglia ed il palazzo dei
Gemelli si sposta al centro, nel fondo. Entra en scena Barbarina, che con lo specchio in mano si pavoneggia tra i due
servi neri.)

Barbarina

Spero diman di far più spicco assai
con la veste ponsò guarnita d'oro.

Smeraldina

(Gridando da fuori scena.)

E lasciatemi entrar!

(Barbarina fa un cenno ai servi, che si spostano ostruendo
l'entrata. Smeraldina entra infilandosi tra i due.)

E lasciatemi entrar; che impertinenza
Sono ormai stanca. Ambasciatori,
memoriali, tornate; ah quante storie!

BRIGHELLA

(Aside.)

Let us make every effort to prolong the life of this lovely antique! But if I don't succeed in having her make a will in my favor, what's it worth to me to have the wreath of Apollo, deep inspiration, poetic passion that envelops me? Unhappy! I see fall from my hands all hope: now not a diamond but just glass!

(Exits, carrying with him a balustrade of one of the palaces. A black servant, in synchronized rhythmical movement with BRIGHELLA, carries off the other balustrade.)

SCENE XIII

(The Palace of KING TARTAGLIA moves off, and the Palace of the twins moves center stage. Enter BARBARINA with a mirror in her hand. She peacocks it between her two black servants.)

BARBARINA

I aim to be more impressive tomorrow
In a red dress trimmed with gold.

SMERALDINA

(Off.)

Let me in.

(BARBARINA makes a gesture to the servants, who take up a place obstructing SMERALDINA's entrance. SMERALDINA forces her way between the two servants and enters.)

Let me enter. What impertinence!
I'm exhausted. Do I have to go
Through a line of ambassadors to see you? What a business!

SMERALDINA

I didn't come here
For your riches,
Love brought me here.

Barbarina

(Fingendo di non riconoscerla.)

Chi è là?

(La riconosce.)

Ah!

Smeraldina

E' il diavol che ti porti.

Barbarina

Temeraria! Sfacciata! Olà, miei servi,
chi vi insegnò a servir? Come si lasciano
penetrare i pitocchi alle mie stanze?

(Fa un cenno ai due servi, che alzano le spade su Smeraldina.
Durante la seguente battuta Smeraldina indietreggia av-
vicinandosi a Barbarina che lancia un grido e s'allontana. Un
tempo dopo i servi calano le spade su Smeraldina che manda
un grido e si sposta rapidamente, evitando per un filo i colpi
di spada. Questa pantomima si ripete per altre due volte nel
corso delle battute, in punti logici.)

Smeraldina

Ah, fraschetta, pettegola, smorfiosa,
madama fricandò, che credi? Forse
di pormi soggezion? Io son qui giunta,

BARBARINA

(Pretending not to recognize her.)

Who is there?

(Recognizing her.)

Ah!

SMERALDINA

(Staring down the servants.)

The devil take you!

BARBARINA

(To SMERALDINA.)

How brash! How shameless!

(To servants.)

Who taught you to serve? Why do you let
Enter riffraff into my presence?

(She gestures to the two servants, who raise their sabres over
SMERALDINA. During the following speeches, SMERAL-
DINA runs to BARBARINA, who lets out a cry and moves away.
A moment later the servants again raise their sabres, SMERAL-
DINA emits a cry and runs about rapidly, escaping a slash and a
blow of their sabres. This pantomime is repeated in the course
of the speech.)

SMERALDINA

Ah, you little fool! Chatterbox! Snob!
Madame fake. What are you thinking of?
Perhaps to embarrass me? I didn't come here

Smeraldina

non per le tue ricchezze, ma l'amore
m'ha trascinata.
Ah, convien ch'io ti baci, ch'io ti mangi.

Barbarina

Ma, viva il ciel, qual confidenza è questa?
Miei servi, dico. (Qui un servo) Incauti! Qui recate
tosto una borsa d'oro, ed a costei
si consegni, e si scacci.

> (I servi si fermano nel centro della scena, quindi escono e
> ritornano con un grande sacco giallo che gettano ai piedi di
> Smeraldina.)

Smeraldina

Barbarina, tu scherzi, è ver? Non mi farai l'affronto
di scacciarmi da te.

Barbarina

Prendi, prendi quell'oro. L'amor tuo
so che s'ammorzerà dentro quell'oro.

Smeraldina

Barbarina t'inganni; io spero ancora
che non discaccerai chi per diciott'anni
t'allevò, chi non ha colpa,

(SMERALDINA)

For your riches,
Love brought me here.
Ah, it maddens me that I came here to kiss you.

BARBARINA

Heavens! What kind of familiarity is this!
Servants come here.

(To SMERALDINA.)

Such audacity!

(To servants.)

Bring me
Here a purse of gold and give it to this woman
And then throw her out.

(The servants exit and return with a big yellow sack of gold
which they throw at the feet of SMERALDINA.)

SMERALDINA

Barbarina, you are joking aren't you? You wouldn't insult
Me by throwing me out.

BARBARINA

Take it, take the gold. I know that your love
Will be extinguished at the sight of it.

SMERALDINA

Barbarina, you are wrong. I still hope
That you will not throw out of your house one who with
   simple love — for eighteen years
Raised you in hers. It wasn't my fault

Smeraldina

se discacciata fosti; chi non fece
altro che lagrimar la tua partenza

Barbarina

Prendi quell'oro, Smeraldina, e parti.
Servi, dal guardo mio costei si levi
a forza.

(I servi alzano lentamente le spade e Smeraldina, terrorizzata, si discosta.)

Smeraldina

Ah, no, servi, pietà. Come signora mia
vi rispetterò sempre. Io non ho cuore
di staccarmi da voi. Tra i vostri servi
la più vil serva reputar mi voglio,
pur ch'io resti con voi. Tenetevi il vostro oro.

Barbarina

(Qual forza ha mia semplicità d'affetti,
tenere espressioni, sul core umano!)
Smeraldina! Resta!
Meco starai, ma le passate cose
mai non rammemorar. Seguimi, e taci.

(Esce di scena.)

Smeraldina

Questa è quella filosofa, che andava
ieri per legna al bosco. ed oggi! . . . basta . . .
Seco volea restar. perchè l'adoro . . .

(SMERALDINA)

You were thrown out. I have been doing
Nothing but crying since you left.

BARBARINA

Take this gold, Smeraldina, and leave.
Servants, take this woman
From my sight.

SMERALDINA

Oh no, servants, have pity on me. As my lady,
I'll respect you always. I have not the heart
To be parted from you. I'll be happy
To be most humble of your servants,
If you'll let me stay near you. Take your gold.

BARBARINA

(Aside.)

It's remarkable the effect her simple
Affection has on the human heart.

(To SMERALDINA)

Smeraldina! Stay!
But if you stay with me never recall
A single moment of the past. Now follow me and shut up!

(Exits.)

SMERALDINA

And this is the philosopher who till
Yesterday went to gather wood in the forest, and now today . . .
   I'll be darned!
I'll stay because I adore her . . .

Smeraldina

Che diavol l'ha arricchita in questa forma?
Io non vorrei che questa frasconcella . . .
Quanta superbia! Ma saprò tutto.

(Dopo aver raccolto il sacco d'oro. Esce.)

SCENA XIV

(Il palazzo dei Gemelli si apre su un giardino, in cui — su un
piedestallo — sta la statua di Pompea. Da sinistra entra Renzo,
che si avvicina, affascinato, alla statua.)

Renzo

No, che donna non v'è che di bellezza
avanzi quella statua, che ebbe forza
di tener fino ad ora questi occhi-fisi
sempre conversi in lei, nel mio giardino,
quanta smania mi sento! Or chi direbbe
che il sprezzator sdegnoso d'ogni donna
caduto fosse in un amoro si ardente
per una donna da scarpello illustre
d'una pietra formata? Ah, tu il dicesti
Calmon, che debolezza in umano core
è grande troppo, e che fra pochi istanti
io proverei qual forza abbia una statua.
Vaglian questi tesori. Io da' confini farò
venir del mondo negromanti,
che diano vita al simulacro amato.
L'oro può tutto: disperar non deggio.

SCENA XV

(Lentamente la reggia dei Gemelli si richiude. Dal fondo della
sala entra precipitosamente Truffaldino.)

98

(SMERALDINA)

I no longer recognize her. What arrogance!
Who the devil has made her so rich?
What snobbishness . . . but I shall find out everything . . .

(Exits.)

SCENE XIV

(The Palace of the twins parts to open on a garden in which, on a pedestal, is a statue of Pompea. Enter RENZO, who approaches the statue.)

RENZO

I've never seen a woman whose beauty
Surpassed that statue in my garden.
It's power keeps my eyes
Transfixed on her.
What is this madness I feel. Who would have thought
It possible that I who had such strong disdain for women
Would fall in ardent love
With a statue by a famous sculptor?
Oh, you said it,
Calmon, the weakness of the human heart
Is too great. In an instant
I have felt the power of a statue.
How I value this treasure. I will call
Wizards from all over the world.
To give life to this beloved statue.
Gold can do everything. I need not despair.

SCENE XV

(Slowly the 'Palace' of the twins reappears. TRUFFALDINO enters precipitously.)

Truffaldino

Oh de casa! . . . Renzo . . . Asino, becco, cornuto!

(Batte violentemente ad una immaginaria porta al lato destro del proscenio.)

Renzo

Mi sembra di sentire la voce di Truffaldino. Non credo che avrà fronte di comparirmi davanti, dopo avermi scacciato.

(Mette la mano ad un'immaginaria maniglia ed apre l'immaginaria porta.)

Truffaldino

Oh, cancar!

(Entrando con violenza. Renzo si ritrae, evitando per poco la porta sul naso.)

A' devi spettà tanto per pudert parlà? El preparà da magnà in tola?

Renzo

Che temerarità è questa? Che sei venuto a fare in questa casa?

Truffaldino

Oh bela per dio. A magnà, bivar e durmì.

Renzo

Hai forse dimenticato di avermi scacciato di casa ier sera con quella asinità?

Truffaldino

Ah, me recordo benissim! L'è proprio una stupida domanda in boca de un filosofo moderno.

TRUFFALDINO

Who's at home ...! Renzo ... Ass, dunce, cuckold!

(He raps violently at the imaginary door to the right side of the proscenium.)

RENZO

I think I hear the voice of Truffaldino. I don't believe he'll have the effrontery to appear before me. After having thrown me out.

(He places his hand on an imaginary door knob and opens an imaginary door.)

TRUFFALDINO

Hey, sourpuss.

(Entering with violence, RENZO withdraws scarcely avoiding getting the imaginary door slammed on his nose.)

I have to wait so long in order to speak to you? Is dinner ready?

RENZO

What kind of impudence is this? Why do you come to this house?

TRUFFALDINO

Oh, for the love of God! To eat, to drink, to sleep, of course!

RENZO

Have you forgotten that you rudely threw me out of your house only yesterday?

TRUFFALDINO

Ah, I remember it very well. What a stupid question in the mouth of today's philosopher.

Renzo

Quale sfrontatezza! Voglio sapere perchè mi hai scacciato di casa.

Truffaldino

Sangue de mi! La cossa l'è chiara co fa una merda de colombo in t'un occhio. Te ho buttà fora de casa perchè ti eri orfano e pitocco.

Renzo

E come mai dopo una simile azione hai cuore di venir a casa mia?

Truffaldino

I m'ha dit che ti è ricco sfondà e mi, co sti vizi e sta fame orba, ho pensà che se pul magnà e sgrafignar un pochetto.

Renzo

Ribaldo e malfattore, non hai vergogna di tale iniquità?

Truffaldino

La xe una vergogna de non vergognarse, perchè i pitocchi i se buta fora de casa e ai ricchi se ghe magna le vissare fin che i deventa pitocchi.

Renzo

Non ho mai sentito un filosofo più franco. Sono voglioso di trattenerlo, ma debbo scacciarlo perchè ha l'animo cattivo.Temerario e sfacciato, vattene tosto o ti farò scorticare vivo come un'anguilla.

(Prende Truffaldino per la collottola, lo spinge sino a sinistra, dove s'immagina una seconda porta, e lo scaraventa fuori con una pedata.)

RENZO

What insolence! I'd like to know why you threw me out.

TRUFFALDINO

Damned be my blood! The thing is as clear as shit of a pigeon in your eye. I threw you out of the house because you were an orphan and penniless.

RENZO

After such an action, you have the gall to come to my house?

TRUFFALDINO

They told me that now you have money without end and since I have a blinding hunger I thought I could eat and fix myself up a little.

RENZO

Swindler! Deceiver! Aren't you ashamed of your iniquity?

TRUFFALDINO

It is a shame, but I'm not ashamed, because penniless people are thrown out of the houses of the rich and because they want to eat at the houses of the rich and eat until the rich become poor.

RENZO

I never heard a more sincere philosopher. I wish I could keep him but he's a bad apple. I'd better get rid of him. Fearless one and shameless one, go away, or I'll have you skinned alive like an eel.

> (He takes TRUFFALDINO by the collar, drags him left where there is an imaginary second door and throws him outside with a kick, slamming the imaginary door.)

Truffaldino

Oh cancar ho fallà nell'ordene. A parlar col cuor in boca l'è andà mal anca con Tartaja. L'è mej cambià musica.

(Passa alla porta di destra e bussa con grazia.)

Renzo abbi un momento de pazienza.
Permesso? . . . Se pol vegnir? . . . Disturbo? . . . No vorrae esser importuno . . .

(Apre la porta, sbattendola sul naso di Renzo che dà un grido di dolore, prende Truffaldino e lo scaraventa fuori. Truffaldino batte con maggiore grazia e chiama:)

Re . . . e . . . e . . . e . . . en . . . zo

(Renzo con l'orecchio dal lato interno della porta e Truffaldino alla stessa altezza dal lato esterno. Gorgheggi di Truffaldino sul nome "Renzo": parte da una nota bassa e sale a toni sempre più alti, quindi scende nota per nota e risale gradualmente a un tono altissimo. Al movimento dei gorgheggi corrisponde un movimento mimico dei due che si alzano o si abbassano lungo la porta, sempre ad ugual altezza. Improvvisamente Truffaldino passa dalla nota altissima ad una molto bassa, per cui Renzo cade a gambe levate. Truffaldino entra, Renzo alzandosi dice:)

Renzo

Che fai Truffaldino, cosa mai ti salta in mente?

Truffaldino

(Girando intorno a Renzo e baciandogli più volte la veste.)

Eccellentissimo, me racomando a la so protezion e ghe baso la vesta. La me conceda, Eccellenza, perdonanza de aver butà fora dai totani

TRUFFALDINO

Oh, dammit, I've made a big mistake. To speak the truth with my heart on my lips is not appreciated. The same happened with King Tartaglia. It is time to sing a different tune.

(He goes to the imaginary door on the right and knocks gently.)

Renzo, have a moment of patience, please. May I? May I come in? Am I disturbing you? I hope I'm not intruding.

(He opens the door, and in so doing bangs it on the nose of RENZO who gives out a cry of pain. RENZO grabs TRUFFAL- DINO and throws him outside. TRUFFALDINO bows with a grand gesture of humility and calls.)

Re...e...e...e...enzo

(RENZO has his door at the ear, and as TRUFFALDINO runs up and down scales on the name of RENZO, going from low to high and back, the two of them with their ears to the door move up and down the door in pantomime. The movements of each correspond with the movements of the other, as TRUF- FALDINO goes down and with going down gets to a very deep note. RENZO falls to the floor. TRUFFALDINO enters, step- ping over RENZO. RENZO jumps up.)

RENZO

Truffaldino, what are you doing? What's on your mind?

TRUFFALDINO

(Moving around RENZO and kissing the hem of his coat.)

Excellency, I came to recommend myself to your protection and I humbly kiss the hem of your coat. Forgive me for having thrown out

Truffaldino

la riosa che co la so spuzza profumegava la me casa che par una catacomba . . .

Renzo

Truffaldino quali stranezze dici mai?

Truffaldino

Mi no son degno, ma el me dev perdunà, perchè in quel punto ero imbriaco chioco, avea el cervelo bislaco, la testa peroca e la boca de un aseno. Me pentisso de le me malefatte e me butto, me prostro a so pie pietosissimi, generosissimi; eccellentissimi . . .

Renzo

Alzati, Truffaldino, non fare lo sciocco.

Truffaldino

Pianzarò tante e tante lacrime sora le so piante fin che non avarò una paroleta de perdono, un sorrisetto de compassion, una sberla che no fassa mal. Digiunarò co fa un remita, me cusirò la boca col spago, starò sempre dur'o, fermo co fa un bacalà. Voj servirla co umiltae fin che no la vedarò morto in cenere, vegnirò a pianze su la so tomba.

> (Descrive col gesto un tumulo ed una croce su cui scrive, pronunciando a soggetto, "Renzo . . . bastardo". Poi raccoglie immaginari fiori in un immaginario prato, dicendo "Rosso, verde, giallo, turchino", Renzo prova a cancellare il nome "bastardo" dalla Croce. Truffaldino gli fa odorare un fiore: Renzo col volto fa cenno che non gli piace; Truffaldino lo butta via e ne sceglie un altro; quindi raccoglie i fiori immaginari in un mazzo che depone con garbo sulla tomba; piange disperatamente ai piedi di Renzo che si commuove e si as-

that rose of a girl who with her bad smell perfumed the house with an oder of the grave.

RENZO

Truffaldino, what strange things are you telling me?

TRUFFALDINO

I beg your forgiveness, because at that time I was drunk. I was out of my mind, I had an empty head and the mouth of an ass. I repent my deeds and throw myself, prostrate, at your feet so full of pity and generosity. Excellency.

RENZO

Truffaldino, don't play the fool. Get up!

TRUFFALDINO

Your Excellency, I shed so many and so many tears at your feet so that you'll have for me a little word of forgiveness, smile of compassion; or even a blow — if it won't hurt too much. I will fast as a hermit, and I will sew up my lips. I'll be still like a salted fish. I'll serve you with humility until I see you dead in ashes and I'll come to cry at your grave.

> (TRUFFALDINO mimes with a jest a gravestone on which he writes, pronouncing softly as he writes "Renzo — the bastard." Then he picks imaginary flowers in an imaginary garden, saying "Red, green, yellow, blue;" RENZO tries to wipe off the name of "bastard" on the tombstone. TRUFFALDINO smells the flowers, RENZO takes one which does not please him and throws it away. TRUFFALDINO pushes him aside and picks another, and while he is picking these imaginary flowers he places them on the grave: he weeps desperately at the feet of

Truffaldino

ciuga le lacrime; leva da tasca un grande fazzoletto inzuppato d'acqua, finge di asciugarsi gli occhi e poi lo strizza con forza, bagnando i piedi di Renzo.)

e a portarghe tanti bei fioretti de tutti i colori e pianzerò, pianzerò . . . Va ben cussì?

Resto balordo; non so capire se Truffaldino sia sciocco o furbo. Voglio tuttavia tenerlo meco, perchè mi diverte.
Truffaldino, così va bene. Se farai come dici, non ti scaccerò.

Truffaldino

El me scusa, eccellentissimo, se no m'ho arecordà de menarlo pel naso, ma me prometo de farlo al pì presto possibile co arte, finezza, e furberia moderna pulita e colta.

Renzo

Truffaldino ha proprio un carattere amenissimo. Servirà per sollevarmi l'animo dalla mia intensa passione; per di più l'aver un buffone è cosa decorosa ad un mio pari.Truffaldino, seguimi.

(Esce.)

Truffaldino

(l'è un gran maledizion no poder mostrarse onesti co le persone che ha pì soldi che sal in zucca).

Renzo

(Da fuori scena.)

Truffaldino!

Truffaldino

Vegno eccellentissimo, subito, ecome qua a menar el da drio.

(Esce.)

RENZO, then he takes a pocket handkerchief from his pocket
and uses it to wipe his tears and then squeezes out the water on
the foot of RENZO, bathing the feet of RENZO — who objects.)

I'll bring so many pretty flowers of so many colors and I will cry and
cry. — How am I doing?

RENZO

I must be a fathead; I don't know if Truffaldino is silly or is astute.
Moreover, he amuses me and I want to keep him with me . . Truffaldino, all right. If you behave as you say, I won't throw you out.

TRUFFALDINO

Please excuse me, Excellency, if I have forgotten to lead you by the
nose, but I promise in the future to do so always with art, finesse,
cunning and guile.

RENZO

Truffaldino really is an amusing character. He will lift my soul from
my intense passion. Moreover, to have a jester is fitting for a man of
my standing. Truffaldino, follow me.

   (Exits.)

TRUFFALDINO

It is a damn shame not to be able to be sincere with people who have
more money than brains.

RENZO

   (offstage)

Truffaldino!

TRUFFALDINO

I'm coming, Excellency, at once, to give you a kick in the ass.

   (Exits.)

SCENA XVI

(Il palazzo dei Gemelli si sposta sulla sinistra ed entra la reggia di Tartaglia a destra. Escono insieme, l'uno dal palazzo e l'altro dalla reggia, Smeraldina e Pantalone con le balaustre e le posano a terra.
La servetta vede Pantalone e rientra precipitosamente.
Il vecchio va a prendere il cannocchiale, guarda il palazzo e poi con il gesto Tartaglia, che entra in scena, assonnato, stirandosi le braccia. Pantalone gli indica il palazzo.)

Tartaglia

Io non so come sia stata questa faccenda. Pantalone, credo di dormire, di sognare, o d'esser a una commedia di trasformazione. Non ho mai creduto che un palagio possa nascere in una notte, come un fungo.

Pantalone

Mo' l'è nato lu, mestà, e de che pegola! E mi povero diavol, vegnindo ier sera a scuro in corte, camminava in pressa, perchè saveva che la piazza gera libera, e ho dà un tossi in tela muraggia de quel palazzo che, se non gaveva sto poco de panza, che me tolesse la botta, fava una fugazza del viso. Chè, ho zavarià mezz'ora a trovare el buso de vegnir a la reggia.

Tartaglia

(Guarda al cannocchiale.)

Gran belle logge! Gran belli colonnati! Gran bella architettura! E' più bella del colosseo di Roma.

SCENE XVI

(The Palace of the Twins is on the left and the Palace of TAR-
TAGLIA is on the right. SMERALDINA and PANTALONE
enter together, at the same time, the one from the Palace of the
Twins and the other from the Palace of the King. Each has a
balustrade and places it, angled, before each of the respective
palaces. The servant SMERALDINA sees PANTALONE and
exits precipitously. PANTALONE goes and takes binoculars;
he looks at the palace gesturing to KING TARTAGLIA, who
comes onstage. He is astonished, flailing his arms. PAN-
TALONE points out to him the palace opposite his own
palace.)

TARTAGLIA

I don't know how this could have happened. Pantalone, I think I'm
sleeping, I'm dreaming, or I'm in a play! I never thought a palace
could grow overnight, like a mushroom.

PANTALONE

But it has been born overnight, Majesty, and of what grandeur! And I,
poor devil, last night, as I was returning to the comfort of the court and
walking in a hurry, believing the square was empty as usual, I bumped
against the wall of that palace. If my belly hadn't softened the blow, I
would have a bump on my forehead. It's not possible! It took me a half
hour to find an opening to get to our palace.

TARTAGLIA

(Looking through the binoculars.)

What a beautiful building! Elegant columns! Great architecture! It is
more beautiful than the Colosseum of Rome.

Pantalone

Bisogna veder i patroni dello stabile, maestà, per farse maravegia.

Tartaglia

Li hai tu veduti? Sono Dei, o diavoli, Pantalone?

Pantalone

Un putto che xe un armellin, una ragazza, che xe un botirro! Maestae, son seguro, che se la vede ghe passa tutte le malinconie.

Tartaglia

Non mi toccar questo punto che mi risveglia il dolor. Non sarà mai vero ch'io lasci di piangere la mia cara Ninetta.

Pantalone

La tasa, che se averze il pergolo.

(Entra in scena Barbarina seguita da Smeraldina.)

La xe giusto quella zogia. La faza grazia, la varda quel tocco.

SCENA XVII

Smeraldina

Il re sopra il verone? Barbarina,
ritiriamoci, andiam via.

Barbarina

Quello è il monarca?
Che importa a me? Di non vederlo io fingo.
Poi non ho soggezione di monarchi.

PANTALONE

You should see the masters of the house, Majesty. You'll be surprised!

TARTAGLIA

Have you seen them? Are they gods, or devils, Pantalone?

PANTALONE

One is a boy! An apricot! And the girl, she's like a piece of butter. I am sure if you see her, you'll stop being melancholy.

TARTAGLIA

Oh, don't bring that up and re-awaken my sorrow. It will never happen that I'll stop crying over my Ninetta.

PANTALONE

Quiet! Their balcony door is opening.

(Enter BARBARINA followed by SMERALDINA.)

She's right there on the balcony. Bow to her, look at that fine, strapping girl.

SCENE XVII

SMERALDINA

Is it the King on his balcony? Barbarina,
Let's withdraw, let's go.

BARBARINA

So! That is the Monarch?
What does he matter to me? I'll feign not to see him.
Besides I'm not in awe of kings.

Tartaglia

Pantalone, Pantalone, che bel viso! Che belle manine! Mi sento brillare il cuore, la malinconia fugge.

Pantalone

Se non gh'è caso, maestae! Co se vede de quei musi, se rallegra anca i indebitai sin alle cege.

Smeraldina

Barbarina, andiam via, che il re vi guarda
col canocchiale. Coi re ci vuol prudenza.

Barbarina

Oh, tu cominci ad essere petulante.
E bene, ho qualchecosa che dispiaccia?
Lascia che guardi pur. Tu vedrai
con una ritirata a tempo, accenderlo
sì che non sappia più quel che si faccia.

Tartaglia

Pantalone, Pantalone, che bel bocchino! Che bel seno! Sento che mi dimentico della quondam Ninetta.

Pantalone

Maestà, mo cossa ghe par de quela conzadura? Del buon gusto de quel vestir?

Smeraldina

Barbarina, andiamo via, andiam via, ch'egli vi tira tanto d'occhiacci addosso. S'ei s'accende,

TARTAGLIA

Pantalone, Pantalone, what a lovely face. What pretty little hands. I feel my heart leaping! My melancholia is gone.

PANTALONE

That's not the way, Majesty! When such faces light up like that they get you in debt right up to the eyebrows.*

SMERALDINA

Let's go! The King is looking at us
Through his binoculars. With kings, one must be prudent.

BARBARINA

Oh, you begin to be overbearing!
So what! Is there something about me that displeases?
Indeed, let him look. You'll see
That with one glance I'll set him on fire
So that he will not know what he's doing.

TARTAGLIA

Pantalone, Pantalone, what a beautiful little mouth. What a beautiful bosom! I feel that I'm forgetting those of Ninetta.

PANTALONE

Majesty, what do you think of that coiffure? Isn't that gown of good taste?

SMERALDINA

Barbarina, let's go, let's go. Now, he's really giving you
The evil eye! He's on fire.

*Translations of the Venetian idioms, (Carla Poli)

Smeraldina

i principi han le mani lunghe assai. Vergognatevi, andiamo.

Barbarina

Oh, tu mi stanchi.
Lascia che s'innamori; è quel ch'io cerco.
Dimmi: non è egli vedovo?

Smeraldina

E, scusate;
Queste son presunzioni troppo grandi . . .

Barbarina

Che! Taci, temeraria; ei non è degno di possedermi.

Tartaglia

Pantalone, sono innamorato come un asino; non posso più; guardami gli occhi, credo di buttar fuoco. Che bella creatura! Vorrei salutarla, vorrei dirle qualche parola, e mi vergogno; ho paura che non mi corrisponda. Sono diventato un bambino all'improvviso, ho perduta tutta la gravità monarchesca.

Pantalone

Come, Maestà? No la se avvilisca; la lo gavarà per onor grando de esser vardada con clemenza de ella; no la daga in ste bassezze de spirito. Un baciamano d'un monarca ha da far buttar zo tremila ragazze dai balconi.

Tartaglia

Mi provo, Pantalone, mi provo.

(SMERALDINA)

Kings have long hands. Shame on you! Let's go.

BARBARINA

Oh, you make me tired.
Let him fall in love. That's what I want.
Tell me: isn't he a widower?

SMERALDINA

Oh! Excuse me!
That's too great a presumption . . .

BARBARINA

Hey! Shut up, you fool! It's *he* who is not worthy of having me.

TARTAGLIA

Pantalone, I'm in love like a fool! I can't take it any longer: look into my eyes. I believe they are afire. What a beautiful creature. I'd like to say hello to her, to say a few words to her, but I'm shy. I'm afraid she may not answer me. I've suddenly become like a child, I've lost all my regal poise.

PANTALONE

How's that, Majesty? Don't let her dishearten you. It would be a great honor for that girl to be looked upon with favor by your Majesty. Do not wallow in low spirits. A kiss on the hand by a king would make three thousand girls fall off a balcony.

TARTAGLIA

I'll try, Pantalone, I'll try.

Pantalone

Ghe raccomando la gravità; maestae.

(Tartaglia fa il gesto di un baciamano molto esagerato, sporgendosi fuori del verone. Pantalone lo trattiene fermandolo in una buffa posa.)

Smeraldina

Noi veniamo alle brutte; ei vi saluta.

Barbarina

Guarda, ed io non mi degno di guardarlo.

(Di scatto volta le spalle.)

Tartaglia

Un buco in acqua, Pantalone, io son disperato.

Pantalone

Mo l'è ben superba quella petaza!

Tartaglia

Non ho più testa; Pantalone; insegnami due parole grandiose di quelle tue veneziane da dirle.

(S'inginocchia.)

Fammi il ruffiano per carità.

Pantalone

(Alzandolo.)

Grazie della carica, maestae. A Venezia se fa l'amore a la francese, o all'inglese; su sto merito no so più niente.

PANTALONE

May I remind you of your rank, Majesty.

(TARTAGLIA makes the gesture of kissing his hand and it's much exaggerated, all the while leaning far out over the balustrade. PANTALONE holds him back in a 'buffo' pose.)

SMERALDINA

We've come to the ugly business. He greets us!

BARBARINA

Look, I don't even condescend to glance at him.

(She turns her back.)

TARTAGLIA

We've just written on water! I'm desperate.

PANTALONE

She has some arrogance, that wench.

TARTAGLIA

I've lost my head, Pantalone. Suggest two grandiose words in your Venetian to say to her.

(He kneels.)

Be my pimp, for pity's sake.

PANTALONE

(Raising him up.)

Thank you for the promotion, Majesty! In Venice, one makes love in French or English: but in this business, I can't help you.

Tartaglia

Aspetta, aspetta; voglio incominciare a introdurmi con spirito e brio.

(Mandando la voce lontano verso il verone opposto.)

Bella giovane, sentite questo scirocco? Ah, Pantalone?

Pantalone

Sior sì; sto introito l'ho sentì mille volte, e l'ha abuo anca spesso un bonissimo esito.

Barbarina

(Imitando la voce di Tartaglia.)

Voi sentite il scirocco, ed a me sembra,
signor che le parole che voi dite
faccian che spiri un'aria molto fredda.

Smeraldina

Uh che insolente! Al re queste risposte!

Tartaglia

M'ha risposto, m'ha risposto con un'insolenza graziosa, Pantalone; e viva. Voglio proseguire con una acuta e gentile proposta; allusiva alla sua bellezza.

(A Barbarina.)

Il sole questa mattina è levato molta risplendente.

Pantalone

Megio: no la gh'ha bisogno de suggeritori, maestae . . . La sa far l'amor che la minia.

TARTAGLIA

Wait, wait. I want to introduce myself with spirit and dash.

(Calling off to the other balcony.)

Beautiful girl, do you feel this warm wind? Ah, Pantalone?

PANTALONE

Yes, sir. I've heard this opening gambit a thousand times, and it ever has had the greatest success.

BARBARINA

(Imitating the voice of KING TARTAGLIA.)

You feel a warm wind, Your Majesty, but to me
The words you're saying
Turn into hot air.

SMERALDINA

Oh, how insolent! What an insult to a King!

TARTAGLIA

She answered me, she answered me with such a delightful insult, Pantalone. Hooray! I want to follow it with a subtle and charming comeback, an allusion to her beauty.

(To BARBARINA.)

The sun rose this morning very resplendently!

PANTALONE

Better: you don't need a prompter, Majesty. You make love like a Casanova.*

---

*The Venetian idiom is too abstruse to be meaningful in English; e.g. as delicately as drawing a miniature.

Barbarina

(A Tartaglia.)

Il sol, che leva risplendente, sire,
non è sempre benefico per tutti.

Pantalone

La ga dà la botta da galantuomo. Oh, l'è navegada sta frascona!

Tartaglia

Oh, che spirito! Oh che diavolino! Ardo tutto, non posso più resistere; bisogna che prenda moglie in secondi voti. Sono tutto allegrezza. Ho piacere di non aver impedimenti e che la quondam Ninetta sia morta. Perdono tutto alla signora madre. Eccola, eccola.

(Entra Tartagliona seguita da Brighella.)

Signora madre, signora madre, la potenza di Cupido m'ha fatto cambiare temperamento; vi voglio bene. Venite a vedere questo mostro di bellezza.

SCENA XVIII

Pantalone

Ih, ih, ih, fogo in camin, fogo in camin.

Barbarina

Che ti par, Smeraldina? A una mia pari
è impossibile che reggano i monarchi.

BARBARINA

(To TARTAGLIA.)

The sun that arises bright, Sire,
Is not always kind to everybody.

PANTALONE

She knows how to give a whack to a suitor. She's been around, that wench.

TARTAGLIA

Ah, what spirit! Oh, what a little devil. I am burning up. I can no longer resist her. I must take a wife a second time. I'm the happiest man in the world. How lucky, nothing stands in my way to marrying her now that Ninetta is dead. All is forgiven to madame, my mother. Her she is, here she is.

(Enter TARTAGLIONA, followed by BRIGHELLA.)

Madame Mother, Madame Mother, the power of Cupid has changed my outlook! I wish you well. Come and see this picture of pulchritude. (He stammers.)

SCENE XVIII

PANTALONE

Ih, Ih, Ih, we're stirring up a bee's nest.

BARBARINA

How is this, Smeraldina?
It's impossible for monarchs to resist anyone the likes of me.

123

Smeraldina

Siete bella, graziosa e ricca assai,
ma che credete alfin? Manco superbia
che qualche cosa mancherà anche a voi.

Barbarina

Nulla a me può mancar; taci, sfacciata.

Brighella

(Piano a Tartagliona.)

Labbra, di questo cor chiavi sicure
non vi scordate i miei funesti accenti

Tartagliona

(Piano a Brighella.)

(Lascia pur far a me). Dov'è oh! mio figlio
quest'oggetto divin ch'ha tanta forza?

Tartaglia

Mirate in ricca e portentosa mole
la bella Aurora, anzi di meriggio il sole.

Pantalone

Porlo esser più cotto? El parla insin colla so rimeta.

Tartagliona

Bella; non so negar.

124

SMERALDINA

You may indeed be beautiful, graceful and rich.
But what do you think will happen to you? I don't have the guts
To tell you that you could possibly lack anything.

BARBARINA

It's not possible that I should lack anything; shut up, impudent one.

BRIGHELLA

(Softly to TARTAGLIONA.)

Lips, which hold fast the key to this heart,
Do not forget my baleful words.

TARTAGLIONA

(Softly to BRIGHELLA.)

Just let me do it. Oh, where is she, my son.
This divine object that has so much power over you?

TARTAGLIA

Look with admiration at the Princess Aurora,
Born of a miracle before the mid-day sun.

PANTALONE

Could one be more head over heels in love? He's talking like a poet.

TARTAGLIONA

Beautiful, yes: I cannot deny it.

TARTAGLIONA

Poet, watch me: I'll finish the deed.

127

Tartagliona

(A Barbarina.)

Figlia, io contemplo
nelle vostre fattezze un bell'oggetto.

(Piano a Brighella.)

Ora le ficco i tuoi detti tremendi.

(A Barbarina.)

"Voi siete bella assai; ma più bella sareste,
s'un dei pomi che cantano, in una mano aveste".

Tartaglia

Uh, che diavol trovate, madre antica?

Pantalone

Questo xe ben cercar el pelo in tel vovo.

Barbarina

E fia possibil, Smeraldina, ahi lassa!
Dunque il pomo che canta io non posseggo?

Smeraldina

Non vel diss'io, che qualcosa vi manca?

Tartagliona

(Piano a Brighella.)

Poeta, attento; l'opera compisco.

(A Barbarina.)

"Figlia, voi siete bella assai, ma più bella sareste
s'acqua che suona e balla, nell'altra mano aveste."

(TARTAGLIONA)

(To BARBARINA.)

Daughter, I am looking at
Your beautiful, gentle features.

(Softly to BRIGHELLA.)

Now I'll nail her with your dreadful words.

(To BARBARINA.)

"You may be beautiful indeed: but you would be more beautiful
If you could have in your hand the apple that sings."

TARTAGLIA

Uh, what devil possesses you, antique mother?

PANTALONE

This indeed is looking for a hair in the egg.

BARBARINA

Is it possible, Smeraldina. How weary!
That there's the apple that sings, and I can't have it?

SMERALDINA

Didn't I just tell you that there would be something that you would
lack?

TARTAGLIONA

(Softly to BRIGHELLA.)

Poet, watch me: I'll finish the deed.

(To BARBARINA.)

"Daughter, you may be beautiful, indeed;
But you would be more beautiful if you were to have in your other
hand the water that sings and dances."

129

Tartaglia

Ohimè, stitica madre, che trovate?

Pantalone

Ghe manca el pomo che canta, e l'acqua che suona e balla? Ghe **ne** indormo alle fantasie de Cappello, barcariol in Piazzetta.

Barbarina

Quai rimproveri a me? Perisca il mondo,
ma non si dica mai, ch'acqua che balla,
ed il pomo che canta, io non possieda.

Smeraldina

E le stelle in guazzetto, ed il sol fritto.

Tartagliona

Figlia, voi siete bella assai, ma più bella sareste
se in possesso l'Augel Belverde aveste.

Tartaglia

Madre inumana, cosa mai voi dite?

Barbarina

Ah no, non può esser! L'Augellin Belverde
dev'esser mio, costi quel che costi.

(Esce di scena con impeto.)

Smeraldina

Ma guarda che fraschetta! Anche l'Augel Belverde.

(Segue Barbarina.)

TARTAGLIA

Oh me, constipated mother, what are you up to?

PANTALONE

Why is that girl envious of the apple that sings and the water that sings and dances?*

BARBARINA

Shall I put up with being talked to like that! Perish the world,
But no one ever is going to say that I didn't possess
The apple that sings and the water that dances and sings.

SMERALDINA

And the stars in a stew, and the sun fried in a frying pan.

TARTAGLIONA

"Daughter, you are beautiful, but you would be more beautiful
If you had in your possession the Green Bird."

TARTAGLIA

Inhuman mother, what are you saying?

BARBARINA

Ah, no, it cannot be! The Green Bird
Must be mine, whatever the cost.

(Exits impetuously.)

SMERALDINA

Just look at that vain girl! And now the Green Bird!

(She follows BARBARINA.)

*Gozzi, Carlo. Opere p. 739.

Brighella

Gran Forza in uman core ha vanitade,
e gran possanza ha poesia sull'alme!

(Esce.)

Pantalone

El fio xe deventà pallido. La marantega giubila;
me cavo dal fresco, che per un poco d'acqua, e un **pomo**,
no vogio esser spettator su sto pergolo de
tragedie, e de sangue tra mare e fio.

(Esce.)

Tartaglia

Madre tiranna, voi non siete paga,
se non fate crepare i vostri parti.

Tartagliona

E che ti feci, figlio temerario?

Tartaglia

Se non foste mia madre . . . Viva il cielo . . .

Tartagliona

Fermati, scellerato, che ti feci?

Tartaglia

Voi per invidia dell'altrui bellezza
mandaste al rischio il mio dolce conforto
di lasciarvi la pelle. Non v'è noto,
qual sia mortal periglio il grand'acquisto
di quel musico pomo, di quell'acqua

BRIGHELLA

What great power has vanity over the human heart!
And great power poetry over the human soul!

PANTALONE

The sun grows dim. The mother looks jubilant:
I'm going to beat it. For a little water and an apple
I don't wish to be a spectator
Of a bloody tragedy between mother and son.

   (Exits.)

TARTAGLIA

Tyrant mother! You don't seem to be satisfied
Unless you snuff out your descendants!

TARTAGLIONA

And what have I done to you, insolent son?

TARTAGLIA

If you were not my mother . . . Oh God in Heaven . . . !

TARTAGLIONA

Stop this minute! Wicked one, what have I done?

TARTAGLIA

Envious of all beauty
You've set my lady-love a task
Where she'll be risking her skin. Don't you know
How mortal is the danger to try to acquire
This musical apple and this water

Tartaglia

d'oro che suona e balla e dell'Augel Belverde?
Che pretendete? Ch'io non abbia moglie?
O che alla fin deva sposar mia madre?
A che mi partoriste? A che nel core
non mi ficcate il spiedo dell'arrosto
e non mangiate le infelici carni
che generaste al mondo? Io maledico
il punto, in cui da un utero sì indegno
nacqui infelice a un scettro, a un trono, a un regno.

(Esce.)

Tartagliona

Purch'io sia salva dal destino oscuro,
che il poeta minaccia,
fremi pur, figlio audace, io non mi curo.

(Fine del primo tempo.)

SECONDO TEMPO
SCENA I

(Si apre il sipario. Il palazzo dei Gemelli è al centro sul fondo.
Il palazzo si apre e appare il giardino con la statua di Pompea.
Entra Renzo.)

Renzo

Oh cara statua, mio candido amore,
parla, dimmi se m'ami, effigie amata.
Tu non muovi le dolci tue labbra,
sei muta e fredda! Perchè non rispondi?
Ma non disse Calmon che nel bisogno
Calmon chiamassi e mi sarebbe amico?
Calmon, Calmon, soccorri un disperato!

(Entra Calmon con lampi e tuono.)

(TARTAGLIA)

Of gold that sings and dances and the Green Bird?
What are you driving at? Because I have not a wife
Is it your plot to have me marry my mother?
And who was it gave birth to me?
Do you want to roast my heart on a spit.
And eat the very flesh that you brought into the world? I curse
The moment in which, from such an unworthy womb,
I, unhappily, was born to a scepter, a throne, and a kingdom!

(Exits.)

TARTAGLIONA

As long as I may be saved from the dark destiny
That my astrologer predicts,
Tremble, indeed, audacious son, I don't care!

ACT II SCENE I

(The stage curtain opens. Upstage and center is the Palace of
the Twins. The Palace opens, and there appears a garden with
the statue of Pompea. Enter RENZO.)

RENZO

Oh, dear statue, my snow-white love,
Speak, tell me that you love me, beloved effigy.
You do not move your sweet lips,
You're silent and cold! Why don't you answer me?
Did not Calmon tell me in case of need
I may call him, and he would be my succor?
Calmon, Calmon, come to the rescue of a desperate man!

(Enter CALMON with thunder and lightning.)

Calmon

Renzo, che vuoi?

Renzo

Calmon ti prego, umilmente ti chiedo
questa statua di sasso di animare!

Calmon

Ma il mio naso non hai restaurato!

Renzo

Calmon perdona ed io ti prometto che il tuo naso ti verrà riparato!
Ma dà la vita alla mia donna amata!

Calmon

Questo nol posso far, Chiedi animata la statua, oggetto del tuo amor,
nè posso compiacerti di ciò. Posso soltanto scior la favella al
simulacro amato per pochi istanti e solo nel periglio.

Renzo

Parlerà meco il sasso? Ah che di tanto
pago sarò, nè più ricerco amico.

Calmon

Ed io ti lascio. Non dimenticar
che il mio naso va riparato. Addio.

(Esce con lampi e tuono.)

Renzo

Oh udire dalle sue labbra i sentimenti

CALMON

Renzo, what is it you wish?

RENZO

Calmon, I pray you, humbly I ask of you
Give life to this statue of stone.

CALMON

But you have not restored my nose.

RENZO

Calmon, forgive me. I promise you that you will see your nose repaired! But do give life to my beloved lady!

CALMON

It is not in my power to do it. For me to ask that the statue, object of your love, come to life! It is not possible for me to grant your request. I am only able to give the gift of speech to the object of your love for a few moments, and only when you are in danger.

RENZO

Will stone speak to me? Ah, for this I will be so
Grateful that I will not ask for more, friend.

CALMON

Now I leave you. Do not forget
That my nose must be repaired. Farewell.

(Exits with lightning and thunder.)

RENZO

To hear from her lips her feelings

Renzo

verso il mio cuor! Deh, se la vista
di quest'occhi beasti, il tuo bel labbro
mandi la voce a ravvivar quest'alma!

Pompea

Il mio nome è Pompea. Di sangue illustre
fu la nascita mia. Diede l'Italia
aura al mio respiro.
Quella vita che vedi, e che più vita
chiamar non posso, sol chiamar si deve
vita, morte, sepolcro e inferno insieme!

Renzo

Dimmi, Pompea, se tu fossi in carne umana,
m'ameresti, o cara?

Pompea

Oh Dio, sì, t'amerei.

Renzo

Tu m'ami? Ahi, voce che il mio cuor rallegri
e laceri in un punto! . . . Ora sei muta?
Deh, parla!!! Pochi istanti Calmon disse,
ora ricordo . . .

(Entra Truffaldino.)

Oh Truffaldino mio!

SCENA II

Renzo

Ah, dimmi, Truffaldino; vedesti mai
più bella creatura della statua

(RENZO)

That do stir my heart! Alas, a glance
From these eyes, sounds from your beautiful lips would revive
  this soul!

POMPEA

My name is Pompea. Of noble blood
Was I born. Italy gave
Breath to my being.
This flicker of life that you now see
That I am no longer able to call life,
I say it's death, the tomb, hell all together!

RENZO

Tell me, Pompea, if you were of flesh and blood again
Would you love me, oh dear one?

POMPEA

Oh, God, would I love you! Yes!

RENZO

You love me? Ah, voice that delights my heart
And tears it apart at the same time . . . Now you're silent?
Alas, speak!!! Calmon said for only a few moments;
Now I remember . . .

SCENE II

(Enter center TRUFFALDINO.)

RENZO

Ah, tell me, Truffaldino; did you ever see
A more beautiful creature than the statue

Renzo

del mio giardin? Di' il ver, non adularmi.

Truffaldino

(Prima della battuta, esce di scena, ritorna immediatamente
con una scala doppia, vi sale, guarda ripetutamente Pompea,
quindi esce con la scala e rientra.)

Dime rufian, se no digo el vero. Verda mo' che pomeline riosa, che
lavrine da basi, che brasseti de butirro, che gambe de piera pomice!
Mi non ho mai visto una femena compagna. (Non ho mai visto in-
vece un mataran simil, che perde le bave per una statua de piera).

Renzo

Chiunque vederà quella bellezza,
di' Truffaldino, non scuserà il mio amore?

Truffaldino

Tuto el contrario! I avarà tuti una invidia marsia, e te tocarà tegnir
ben i oci averti per no deventar cornuto! (Anca mi so sta inamorà de
qualche statua de piera, ma la gaveva le ciape un po' pì tenerete).

Renzo

Ah, che dovrò pensar sulle parole

(RENZO)

In my garden? Tell me the truth, and do not flatter me.

TRUFFALDINO

(Immediately following RENZO's speech, he leaves the stage, returns immediately with a ladder which he climbs up and looks repeatedly at POMPEA, then he leaves with the ladder and re-enters.)

Call me a pimp, if I don't tell the truth. I have never seen such laughing cheeks, such lips wanting to be kissed, arms like butter, legs of pumice stone. I've never seen a woman to compare to her.

(Aside.)

Neither have I ever seen anyone so dimwitted that he slobbers over a statue of stone.

RENZO

Don't you think that whoever saw such beauty,
Tell me Truffaldino, would not excuse my love?

TRUFFALDINO

Quite the contrary! Everybody would be wild with envy, you'd have to keep your eyes open not to become a cuckold.

(Aside.)

Even I have been in love with some statues of stone, but they had buttocks a little bit more tender.

RENZO

Ah, that I must reflect on the words

Renzo

dell'Augel Belverde, che m'apparve,
che negò palesar di chi son figlio?

Truffaldino

Ah, che pensar dell'Osel Belverde
che negò dirme de chin son figlio?
(ha dito che son bastardo, nato da un biro e da una chincagliera de
piazza e che mi mader l'è sta nove mesi a parturirme).

SCENA III

Barbarina

Lasciami, Smeraldina, io non credea
che nulla a me mancasse, e sofferire
non puote, anzi non deve una mia pari
non possedere il pomo virtuoso,
l'acqua che balla e l'Augellin Belverde.

Smeraldina

Ma, cara figlia, se non v'è rimedio!
Chiunque acquistar volle quelle cose,
miseramente è morto; non v'è caso.

Barbarina

Morto o non morto. Facile o difficile,
io devo possedere l'acqua che danza,
e il pomo che canta e l'Augel Belverde!

Renzo

Fuor di se stessa è la sorella mia;

(RENZO)

Of that Green Bird which appeared before me.
He refused to tell me whose son I am.

TRUFFALDINO

Ah, you're thinking of a Green Bird
Who refused to tell you whose son you are?
That bird said I was a bastard, born of a flatfooted porter and a female
peddler in the Piazza, and that my mother took nine months to beget
me!

SCENE III

BARBARINA

Don't bother me, Smeraldina. I didn't believe
I was lacking anything; that it was not possible
For me to suffer the degradation
Of being in want of this exceptional apple, dancing waters,
   and the Green Bird.

SMERALDINA

But dear child, what's to be done?
Whoever undertook to get them,
Unfortunately, died. There is no
      way to get them!

BARBARINA

Death or no death. Easy or difficult,
I must have the waters that dance,
The apple that sings, and the Green Bird!

RENZO

My sister is beside herself:

Renzo

che mai sarà! La vedi, sai tu nulla?

Truffaldino

La sarà incocalia per l'Osel Belverde o per qualche
alter oseleto de bosco, rosso o turchin.

Barbarina

Ah, Renzo, ah, mio fratello, io son nel mondo
più sfortunata di qualunque donna,
un oggetto da nulla, il scherno, il riso,
il lubidrio d'ognuno che mi guarda.

Renzo

Che t'avvenne, sorella? Quale sventura?
Che dici mai? Questo non è possibile.

Barbarina

E' possibil purtroppo. il raro albergo,
e le immense ricchezze d'oro e gioie
e la bellezza che possiedo, e i servi
non vaglion nulla. Fui rimproverata
di non aver l'acqua che balla, e il pomo
che canta, in mano, e l'Augellin Belverde!
Ti par poco
questa disgrazia mia? Deh, Renzo amato,
per quanto ami la vita della suora,
non mi lasciar senza i due rari oggetti;
che indispensabil cosa è il possederli.

Truffaldino

L'acqua che balla e i pomi che canta

(RENZO)

That will never do! Look at her, can't you do something?

TRUFFALDINO

She has to become infatuated with a Green Bird? Why not some other
bird of the forest, red or blue.

BARBARINA

Ah, Renzo, ah, my brother, in the whole world
I am the most unfortunate girl!
I'm nothing, a mockery, a joke,
A laughing stock for all to see.

RENZO

What has happened to you, sister? What misfortune?
What ever are you saying? It's not possible.

BARBARINA

It is more than possible. This exceptional palace,
The immeasurable wealth of gold and jewels,
The beauty I possess and the servants,
All are worth nothing. I've been scorned for not having
    in my hand the water that dances, the apple
That sings, nor the Green Bird!
Can't you see
That for me this is a disgrace? For pity's sake, beloved brother!
If you care for the life of your sister,
Do not allow me to go on without these two rare things;
It is a matter of life and death that I have them.

TRUFFALDINO

Waters that dance, an apple that sings!

Truffaldino

le xe certo cosse pì necessarie
del pan che se magna.

Renzo

Ma, Barbarina, non sapete, come
queste cose acquistar non è possibile!
E a certa morte corre chi al gran rischio
si mette ad acquistarle? Ah, vanerella,
apri quegli occhi, e del fratel la vita
ti stia più a cor d'una poca d'acqua e un pomo.

Barbarina

Ah, barbaro fratello! io ben sapeva,
che non m'amasti mai. Serva, sostienimi . . .

(Si mette in posizione per svenire, attende che Smeraldina sia
pronta per sostenerla, quindi si lascia andare nelle braccia
della serva.)

Già mi palpita il cuor . . . mi gira il capo . . .
tutta convulsa io son . . . sugli occhi un velo . . .
m'abbarbaglia la vista . . .

(Improvvisamente si drizza e s'avvicina al fratello.)

Ti ricorda,
fratel, che aveste cuore a una sorella
l'acqua, e il pomo negar,

(Si rimette in posizione per svenire e ricade nelle braccia di
Smeraldina, dicendo:)

per se muore.

Smeraldina

Barbarina, mia cara, via coraggio
de' non morite . . .

(TRUFFALDINO)

Yes, they are certainly more necessary
Than the bread we eat!

RENZO

But Barbarina, don't you know
That it is not possible to get these things!
It's certain death for whoever takes the great risk
To get them. Ah, vain one,
Open your eyes and let the life of your brother
Be more dear to your heart than a little water and an apple!

BARBARINA

Oh! Cruel brother! I knew you never loved me.
Servant, catch me!

> (She places herself in a position to faint, waits until SMERAL-
> DINA is ready to support her, then she lets herself fall into her
> arms.)

My heart palpitates . . . My head swims . . .
I'm having convulsions . . . A thickness veils my sight.
I see spots before my eyes . . .

> (Suddenly she straightens up and confronts her bother.)

Remember,
Brother, that you had the heart to deny to a sister
Water and an apple!

> (She returns to fainting in the arms of SMERALDINA.)

And to let her die.

SMERALDINA

Barbarina, my dear one! Courage!
Do not die!

147

Truffaldino

Oh, poareta, ghe casca el fià, la xe bianca
palida co fa un cadavere. I sali, i sali.

Renzo

Or tutto intendo. Ecco i perigli, ch'io
non devo ricusare, per quanto disse
l'Augel Belverde, ed ecco del pugnale
chiaro l'arcano. Io dar principio deggio
all'imprese tremende, per le quali
deve aver vita, il simulacro amato.
Sorella, ti conforta; o il raro pomo
e l'acqua e l'Augel avrai fra poco.
e tuo fratello non sarà più vivo.

Barbarina

(Improvvisamente normale, si drizza e s'avvicina a Renzo.)

Respiro, oimè, fratello, ti ringrazio;
deh, non morir, ma acquista il pomo, l'acqua
e l'Augel Belverde.

Renzo

(Trae un pugnale.)

Questo lucido ferro tu conseva
io vado ad appagarti.
In sin ch'egli risplende,
vive il fratello tuo; se egli apparisce
lordo di sangue, tuo fratello è morto.
Truffaldino, mi sequi a questa impresa.

TRUFFALDINO

Poor little thing. She had the vapors! She's as white and pale as a
corpse. Smelling salts! Smelling salts!

RENZO

Now I understand everything. This is the danger,
That I must not avoid: so says
The Green Bird; and this is the mystery
Of the bright dagger. I must begin
At once this tremendous enterprise; for in such a way
Have I to give life to my beloved statue.
Sister, be comforted. Either I'll get the rare apple,
The water and the Green Bird,
Or I will not be among the living anymore.

BARBARINA

(Suddenly alert and wide-awake, she advances to RENZO.)

Alas, I breathe again, brother, I thank you.
Pray, don't die. But get me the apple, the water
And the Green Bird.

RENZO

(He draws the dagger.)

Keep this shining dagger
With you while I'm gone.
While it shines,
Your brother is alive, but if you see it stained
With blood, your brother is dead.
Truffaldino, follow me in this enterprise.

Truffaldino

(Fa un giro della scena, inseguito da Renzo.)

No poss propri, ho un calo che me diol troppo.

Renzo

Seguimi, o in casa mia, più non venire.

(Esce.)

Truffaldino

Cantarae vulantiera 'na cansoneta, ma ho el naso
che me cola pel rafredor!

(Esce.)

Barbarina

Ho vinto, Smeraldina. Al ciel si mandino
preci divote. Ricchi sacrifizi
faremo ai numi. I numi la brama
appagheranno, e non vorran ch'io resti
mortificata, e dì men funesti.

Pompea

Barbarina, t'affretta,
Tuo fratello è morto.

Smeraldina

Ohimè, quel simulacro ha ragionato.

TRUFFALDINO

(Stalling, takes a turn about the stage and follows RENZO.)

No! I can't! I have a corn! It hurts me too much.

RENZO

You'll follow me, or I'll kick you out of my house.

(Exits.)

TRUFFALDINO

I'd gladly sing a little song, but I have a cold and my nose is running!

(Aside.)

Thinking it over, I'd better follow him. I don't want to be stuck in a house of masters who are very rich but crazy! With their lack of brains, they'll soon become very poor. I could sing an aria about that, but I've got a cold and my nose keeps running.

(Exits.)

BARBARINA

I've won. Smeraldina! To heaven we'll raise
Our prayers and make rich sacrifices
To the gods, for they will satisfy my longing.
They do not want me to be
Mortified, or at the very least sad!

POMPEA

Barbarina, hurry!
Your brother is near death!

SMERALDINA

O, me! The statue has spoken!

Barbarina

Morto è il fratel? Che narri, eh, stolta. Taci.
Terso è il pugnale, mio fratello è in vita.

Pompea

Indiscreta, superba. Adunque aspetti,
che sanguinoso
apparisca il pugnal, per poi dolerti
invan della miseria del tuo sangue?

Smeraldina

La statua dice bene. Siete matta.

Barbarina

Dunque dovrò soffrir di non sapere
chi sieno i genitor? Dovrò soffrire
i rimproveri altrui? Non sarò degna
per non avere un Augellin Belverde
d'esser sposa al monarca? Ah, si vuol troppo.

Pompea

Ferma il fratello, o invan lo piangerai.

Barbarina

La voce di costei nel cor mi passa;
tutta mi fa tremar . . . Son disperata.
Ah, si salvi il fratel; dell'altra brama
forse m'appagherò. Serva, mi segui;
verso il colle dell'Orco io movo il piede.

(Esce.)

BARBARINA

My brother dead? Who says so? Oh, such foolishness, be
  silent.
Brilliant is the dagger, my brother is alive.

POMPEA

Imprudent and haughty one. Are you waiting
For blood
To appear on the dagger so that then you may weep
In vain over the agony of one of your own blood?

SMERALDINA

The statue is telling you! Barbarina, you're crazy not to heed
  her.

BARBARINA

Must I endure not knowing
Who were my parents? Must I bear
The reproaches of others? Am I not
To have a Green Bird?
Become the wife of a king? Ah, you ask too much of me.

POMPEA

Go to your brother, or you'll cry for him in vain.

BARBARINA

Her words cut through my heart;
She makes me tremble . . . I am desperate.
Ah, brother, save yourself! Perhaps
I will get them myself. Servant, follow me;
I make my way to the mountain of the Ogre.

> (Exits.)

E pur è ver. Quando si vuol del bene
a una persona, non ci si può staccar;
e, quantunque sia matta da catene,
sino al colle dell'Orco ella si segua.
Sarà per amor proprio. Pazienza.

(Esce.)

SCENA IV

(Esce il palazzo dei Gemelli ed entra la grotta. Contemporaneamente vengono in scena due mimi vestiti da alberi orrendi, l'albero con la testa di pomo, l'Augellin Belverde e cinque ballerine vestite di acqua azzurra, i quali mimano una scena di vita felice nel bosco. Durante le battute della Fata Serpentina, essi, seguendo il ritmo del verso, man mano si pongono in questa disposizione: le Acque, all'entrata della grotta; gli alberi mostruosi, alla sinistra della grotta; l'Augellin, al lato sinistro sopra un piedistallo, il Pomo alla destra della stessa.)

Voce di Fata Serpentina

O voi che l'arboscello dei miei pomi guardate
grotta che l'acque bevi, danzatrici dorate,
nuove insidie vi giungono; tenete aperti gli occhi
sicchè l'acqua ed i pomi nessun mortale tocchi.

Renzo

(Entra Renzo con la spada in mano, Truffaldino dietro di lui, inciampa. Terrore di Renzo che subito si riprende e zittisce il servo.)

Oh, quale bosco orrido! dev'essere proprio questo il colle dell'Orco.

SMERALDINA

How too true it is. Even when she wishes
Well she cannot forget about her self!
Although Barbarina is stark raving mad
I must follow her to the mountain of the Ogre.
So this is for "love of One's self?" Patience, Smeraldina.

(Exit.)

SCENE IV

(The Palace of the Twins changes to the grotto. Enter two
mimes as monster trees, the tree with the apple, the Green Bird,
and five ballerinas dressed as blue waters; they mime a happy
life in the woods. During the speech of Fata Serpentina the
above move in rhythm to the verse: they are placed thus: the
five waters at the entrance to the grotto; the trees to the left of
the grotto; the Green Bird to the left on a pedestal; the apple tree
to the right of the Green Bird.)

VOICE OF FATA SERPENTINA

Oh, you young apple tree, keep
From the grotto those who would drink the waters, dancers beloved
New snares are set. Keep your eyes open
That no one mortal may touch the water and the apples.

(Enter RENZO with sword in hand, TRUFFALDINO to right
stumbles, and frightens RENZO, who then turns suddenly and
bumps into TRUFFALDINO.)

RENZO

O, what a horrible forest. It must indeed be the mountain of the Ogre.

Truffaldino

Porco de mi. L'e propri questo! (L'è tanto scuro che no ghe vedo una maledetta).

> (I due fanno un giro della scena. E' buio pesto ed essi non riescono a scorgere alcuna casa. Renzo senza avvedersene infila la spada sotto il braccio di Truffaldino, il quale crede di essere stato trafitto da una spada magica e cade a terra, convinto di essere morto. Renzo accorre per aiutarlo, lo guarda, s'accorge di non avere più nella mano la spada, si china su di lui, cercando di alzarlo, ma non s'avvede che in questo movimento infila sotto il suo braccio la stessa spada. Anch'egli pensa di essere stato ferito. Accorre Truffaldino, prende l'elsa con tutte e due le mani, estrae con forza l'arma e quindi osserva attentamente la lama per vedere se c'è del sangue. Renzo, dopo aver constatato che nessuna ferita c'e nel suo petto, riprende la spada e fa cenno a Truffaldino di seguirlo. I due girano intorno agli alberi, l'uno a destra e l'altro a sinistra. Non riescono a scorgere nulla. Le loro mani si muovono tra i rami, senza mai toccarli. I due, dopo un giro, si scontrano al centro della scena, danno un forte urlo di terrore; quindi si toccano il viso reciprocamente, riconoscendosi. Renzo vede finalmente l'entrata della grotta e si ritira spaventato verso il proscenio, a destra. Truffaldino lo segue.)

Renzo

Truffaldino, quella è la grotta ove si dice sia rinchiusa l'acqua che balla e suona.

Truffaldino

(S'avvicina alla grotta per guardare, poi ritorna verso Renzo.)

(L'è mejo darghe razon ai mati).

TRUFFALDINO

I'll be damned! It's the very place! It's so dark I don't see a damned thing.

(The two do a turn around the stage. It's dark and they don't find anything. RENZO, not having seen anyone, accidentally inserts his sword under the arm of TRUFFALDINO, whereupon TRUFFALDINO thinks he's been stabbed by a magic sword and falls, convinced he's dead. RENZO runs to aid him, looks at him, realizes he no longer has in his hand his sword, bends over TRUFFALDINO seeking to raise him. At that moment the same sword gets thrust under his arm, and he thinks he's been wounded. TRUFFALDINO runs to him, pulls it out, looks carefully to see if there is blood. None. RENZO, now assured that no one has wounded him, takes up the sword and orders TRUFFALDINO to follow him. The two move among the trees, one to the right, the other to the left. They don't find anything. Their hands move among the branches without ever touching anything. The two circle and then bump into each other, uttering cries of terror. Once they touch each other's faces, they recognize each other. RENZO finally enters the grotto; he runs out; frightened. TURFFALDINO follows him.)

RENZO

Truffaldino, that is the grotto where the waters dance and sing.

TRUFFALDINO

(He draws close to the grotto; then returns to RENZO.)

(Aside.)

It's better to agree with the crazy!

RENZO

Don't you hear singing and playing?

TRUFFALDINO

It's my hungry stomach grumbling like a boiling pot of beans.

Truffaldino

Certo l'è questa!

Renzo

Vedi i pomi che pendono da quell'albero? Quelli sono i pomi che
cantano.

Truffaldino

(S'avvicina al pomo. Cerca con le mani. Il pomo evita, con
rapidi spostamenti delle braccia, di essere toccato. Truffaldino ritorna a Renzo.)

(Sarò orbo, ma no ghe vedo gnanca a biastemiar). Belli quei pomi!!!

Renzo

Truffaldino, il momento è assai grave. Senti tu canti e suoni?

Truffaldino

(Si sposta al centro, tendendo le orecchie per udire, ora di qua,
ora di là.)

Sento tutta la sinfonia dei anzoli del Paravis.
(L'è el mio stomego che brontola dalla fame, co
fa una pignatta de fagioli de bojo).

Renzo

Pensi Truffaldino che ci siano pericoli?

(TRUFFALDINO)

(To RENZO.)

Certainly, that's the place!

RENZO

Do you see apples hanging from that tree? Those are the apples that sing.

TRUFFALDINO

(He advances to the apple; grabs for it. The apple escapes him with a rapid movement of its branches. TRUFFALDINO returns to RENZO.)

(Aside.)

I must be blind, but I swear I don't see a thing.

(To RENZO.)

O, what beautiful apples!!!

RENZO

Now, really, this moment is momentous. Don't you hear singing and playing?

TRUFFALDINO

(Moving center, cocking his ears to hear now left, now right.)

I hear a symphony of angels in paradise!

(Aside.)

It's my hungry stomach grumbling like a boiling pot of beans.

RENZO

Do you think we are in danger?

Truffaldino

Gnente, nissun perigol. L'è fiabe per puteli, perchè no i vegna a robar i pomi.

Renzo

Truffaldino, guarda intorno se vedi fiere, draghi, orchi, serpenti.

Truffaldino

Vardo.

(Cerca per terra, come per trovare degli insetti.)

No vedo gnanca una formigola.

(Improvvisamente si trova davanti al Pomo e si ritira spaventato.)

Oh, adesso li vedo! Ghe xè solo un albero de pomi!

Renzo

Entra dunque in quella grotta e riempi l'ampolla d'acqua.

Truffaldino

Pronti, la impenisso in un momento.

(Andando velocemente verso il Pomo. Il Pomo viene avanti, danzando, in atteggiamento minaccioso. Truffaldino si ferma e indietreggia.)

Voce

O cupidigia umana.
Quando paga sarai?
Deh, fuggi e t'allontana.
Goditi quello ch'hai
nè ricercar di più.

TRUFFALDINO

Not at all; no one is in danger. It's a fairy story for children so they won't steal apples.

RENZO

Truffaldino, look inside to see if there are animals, dragons, witches, serpents.

TRUFFALDINO

I'm looking.

(Looking on the ground as if to find insects.)

I don't see even an ant.

(Suddenly he finds himself in front of the apple tree and he withdraws scared.)

Oh, now I see them. It's only an apple tree.

RENZO

Then go into the grotto and fill this bottle with water.

TRUFFALDINO

Ready. I'll get it in a moment.

(Going rapidly toward the apple tree. The apple tree comes towards him, dancing, menacingly. TRUFFALDINO falls back.)

VOICE

O, greedy ones!
When will you pay for your sins?
Go, flee far away.
Enjoy what you have.
Don't ask for more.

Truffaldino

(Ritirandosi precipitosamente verso Renzo.)

Renzo, i pomi s'ha messo a cantar. Com'ela sta stravaganza?

Renzo

Balordo, che meraviglia ti prende? Corri e va a spiccare uno di quei pomi.

Truffaldino

(Si avvia ancora verso il Pomo, che ora è al centro del palcoscenico.)

Vado e cercherò de toir quello che compatisse la mia anima innamorata.

(Nelle battute seguenti si avrà un'allegra pantomima di Truffaldino che cerca invano di predere l'albero che scivola via veloce.)

Eccolo! Vojo quello più rosso de tutti. Ho paura ch'el sia una poma. Fermo co le man. Tira zo quell'altra!

Renzo

Presto, Truffaldino, cerca di afferrare il pomo!

Truffaldino

Oh, ste rame le gh'ha el rebegolo!

Renzo

Su, Truffaldino, sii veloce!

Truffaldino

Più del vento. El scampa! Oh diavol, el par un bisato!

(Il Pomo dà un colpo con un ramo sulla testa di Truffaldino.)

Aiuto che gnocca!

TRUFFALDINO

(Backing up precipitously toward RENZO.)

The apples have started to sing! Is this a nightmare?

RENZO

Fathead! What's the matter with you? Run and pick one of those apples.

TRUFFALDINO

I'll go, scared out of my wits, and try to get one.

(He tries to grab one, but the tree moves its branches away.)

I want the reddest one of all. I'll bet it's just an apple. I'll grab it with my hand. Now, I'll try to get the other one.

RENZO

Quick, Truffaldino. Try to get one.

TRUFFALDINO

Oh, that branch has St. Vitus' dance.

RENZO

Quick! Be fast, Truffaldino!

TRUFFALDINO

It gets away like the wind. Oh the devil, it's like an eel.

(The apple raps TRUFFALDINO on the head.)

Help!

(To RENZO.)

Blockhead!

Renzo

Sciocco, vedrai che lo spicco io il pomo!

(Arditamente fa per affrontare il Pomo, ma viene preso dai rami di uno dei due alberi mostruosi.)

Truffaldino

Gnente paura! Saldo in poppe, arrivo mi.

Renzo

Attento Truffaldino!

Truffaldino

(Viene afferrato dal secondo albero mostruoso.)

Me par de essere un oseleto. Fe' pian bastardi, che gh'ho un callo! Aiuto son morto!

Renzo

Calmon, Calmon, soccorri un disperato!

Calmon

(Lampi e tuono; Calmon entra da destra.)

Dov'e filosofia? Renzo che fai?

Renzo

Simulacro, fa' ch'io acquisti il disiato pomo e l'acqua rara!

Calmon

Si, ma prima la promessa da te chiedo:
Ancora questo naso non m'hai restaurato!

RENZO

Fool! I see that I shall have to pick the apple!

(He tries to grab the apple, but the two monster trees prevent it.)

TRUFFALDINO

Nothing to fear! Take a stand! I am coming.

RENZO

Careful, Truffaldino!

TRUFFALDINO

(Getting caught by the second tree.)

I feel like a little bird. Take it easy, bastard, I've a corn on my toe. Help, I'm dying.

RENZO

Calmon, Calmon! Come to the help of a desperate man!

CALMON

(Lightning and thunder.)

Where is your philosophy, Renzo? What are you doing?

RENZO

Statue, help me get the much needed apple and the rare waters.

CALMON

Yes, but first: what about the promise that I exacted from you? You still have not restored my nose!

Renzo

Oh, si Calmon, io tel prometto e giuro!

Calmon

Da tanto tempo ancora non l'hai fatto.

Renzo

Aiutami, Calmon. Non mancherò!

(Lampi e tuono.)

Calmon

Guarda il tuo servo: ei no è morto!

(Lampi e tuono. L'albero mostruoso allenta i suoi rami e Truffaldino cade pesantemente al suolo.)

Truffaldino

(Suo risveglio, afferrando comicamente le parti del suo corpo che va elencando. Poi si alza.)

Hojo ancora la testa, le gambe, i brazzi, el stomegeto, el cuor? Sangue de mia mader chincagliera de piazza, m'ho insonnià de esser in una boscaglia piena de brutti musi che facea paura e de cadaveri messi a mucchio, davanti a una grotta. Quel bastardo de Renzo volea chiappà un pomo . . .

(Senza accorgersi si avvicina a Calmon.)

Calmon

Il pomo acquisterai!

Truffaldino

Aiuto, la voce de una manza!

(Si ritrae spaventato e si trova davanti gli alberi mostruosi.)

Aiuto i brutti musi!

RENZO

Oh, yes. I promise and swear to do it.

CALMON

So long ago and you haven't done it yet.

RENZO

Help me, Calmon. I will not fail you!

(Lightning and thunder. The monster tree raises its branches and TRUFFALDINO falls heavily to the earth.)

CALMON

Look at your servant: he is not dead!

TRUFFALDINO

(Taking count of the parts of his body. Then he rises.)

Have I still my head? legs? arms? stomach? heart? Blood of my mother who peddled in the Piazza. I was dreaming of being in a wood full of ugly mugs piling up bodies before a cave. How it frightened me! And that bastard Renzo wanted me to reach for an apple.

CALMON

You will get the apple.

TRUFFALDINO

Help! The voice of a bull!

(He withdraws frightened and finds himself before the monster trees.)

Help! Those ugly mugs!

Truffaldino

(Fugge, riparandosi dietro a Calmon. Lampi e tuono.)

Calmon

T'avvicina all'albero fatal e spicca il pomo!

Renzo

Oh generoso, io pronto t'obbedisco.

(Renzo s'avvicina all'albero e stacca un pomo.)

Ecco il pomo. Oh, gioia!

Calmon

Dell'acqua io vo che prenda.
Entri il servo alla grotta e non paventi
ivi raccolga l'acqua e non paventi!

Renzo

Su, briccone, fatti cuore ed entra!

Truffaldino

Son deventà un cadavere marcio anca mi!

Renzo

Canaglia, ingrato! Entrerai a colpi di bastone sulla schiena.

Truffaldino

A vaghi!

(TRUFFALDINO)

(He runs, placing himself behind CALMON.)

(Lightning and thunder.)

CALMON

Approach that deadly tree and pick the apple.

RENZO

O, kind-hearted! I'll obey at once.

(He approaches the tree to take an apple.)

Here is the apple. O, joy!

CALMON

I want you to take some water.
Have the servant enter without fear the grotto
And get the water without fear.

RENZO

Quick, simpleton! Be of strong heart and enter.

TRUFFALDINO

I'll become a rotten corpse, that I will!

RENZO

Silly goose, ingrate! You'll enter, or with my stick I'll rain down blows
on your back!

(Music: then the waters come dancing out of the grotto.)

TRUFFALDINO

In I go!

Truffaldino

(Fa per avviarsi, ma si ferma improvvisamente si volta e s'inginocchia.)

Ah, Truffaldino, più non vederai el lome del sol
che vago poggia i suoi rai su le luganeghe.
Più magnarò quelle fette de lardo
delle cucine de Renzo bastardo!

Renzo

Avanti, entra vile servo!

Truffaldino

(S'avvia tremante, si ferma devanti alle Acque. Qui ha luogo, durante le battute seguenti, un'allegra pantomima, in cui Truffaldino mima la scena di uno che cade in acqua, lotta con le onde e sta per esser sopraffatto dalla forza degli elementi.)

A non son bon de nuotare!

Renzo

Su, fatti cuore, prendi l'acqua! Non c'è alcun pericolo!

Truffaldino

Son cascà in canalazzo!

Renzo

Non temere, afferrala!

Truffaldino

Aiuto! Me annego, me soffego, me manca el fià.
dame una man!

Calmon

Si fermi l'acqua e segua il servo!

(Lampi e tuono. Le Acque si fermano e si ritraggono, lasciandosi condure dolcemente come un gregge di pecore. Truffaldino si diverte a bagnarsi le mani.)

172

(TRUFFALDINO)

(He draws near, but suddenly stops, turning and lies down.)

Ah, Truffaldino, you'll never see again the light of the sun which gently lays its rays on sausages, never to eat those slices of bacon from the kitchen of Renzo the Bastard!

RENZO

Go on, enter, you faint-hearted slave.

TRUFFALDINO

(Mimes falling in the middle of the waters.)

I'm no good at swimming.

RENZO

Hurry! Take heart! Get the water! There's no danger.

TRUFFALDINO

I've fallen in the Grand Canal!

RENZO

Stop being afraid! Get the water.

TRUFFALDINO

Help! I'm drowning, I'm choking, I'm out of breath. Give me a hand.

CALMON

Water, stop! and come back servant.

(Lightning and thunder. The waters stop and withdraw and follow TRUFFALDINO. TRUFFALDINO clowns washing his hands among the waters.)

Renzo

Oh, gioia, Truffaldino. L'acqua è in nostro possesso.

Truffaldino

Oh, che bella acquetta! Me bagno le man! Me le asciugo sul cuor.

Calmon

La foresta s'acquieti, la pace ancor regni
nel giardin di Fata Serpentina.

(Lampi e tuono. Calmon s'avvia ad uscire.)

Renzo

Calmon, Calmon!!

Voce di Calmon

Renzo che vuoi?

Renzo

Calmon, dà vita alla mia amata statua!

Voce di Calmon

Io nulla posso far. Questo è l'arcano
ch'è dipendente dall'Augel Belverde!
Fa che il mio naso sia restaurato
e avrai possesso dell'Augel Belverde!

(Lampi e tuono. Calmon sparisce.)

Renzo

Calmon, Calmon!!!

RENZO

Oh, joy, Truffaldino, the water is in our possession!

TRUFFALDINO

Oh, what beautiful water. I wash my hands. I dry them over my heart.

(With his hand on the heart patch on his behind.)

CALMON

The forest is quiet, peace reigns again
In the garden of Fata Serpentina.

(Lightning and thunder. CALMON starts to leave.)

RENZO

Calmon, Calmon!

VOICE OF CALMON

Renzo, what do you want?

RENZO

Calmon, I beg of you to give life to my beloved statue.

VOICE OF CALMON

I cannot help you in this. That magic
Depends on the Green Bird.
Have my nose restored!
And get possession of the Green Bird!

(Lightning and thunder. CALMON exits.)

RENZO

Calmon! Calmon!

Truffaldino

Sangue de mi, andemo a comprar un naso!

Renzo

Oh, Truffaldino mio, tre mila miglia
è lontana la città da questo luogo.
Io vo' da solo a catturar l'Augello.

Truffaldino

Cattura, cattura pur da solo! Mi te aspetto qua.

Renzo

Ma che bado a costui? Le mie premure
non ammettono ritardi: a che mi fermo?

(S'avvia verso l'Augellino.)

Truffaldino

Adesso salta fuora l'orco o qualche alter cossa. Nassarà disgrazie
grandi! Vegnerà fora qualche mostro grando.

(L'Augellin si fa incontro minaccioso. Renzo tenta tre volte di
afferrarlo. Invano. Quindi l'Augellin lo tocca e Renzo si
tramuta in statua di sasso.)

Renzo

O dio, che sento? Ah, che doglia . . . Oh, angoscia . . .

Truffaldino

(S'avvicina a Renzo. Lo tocca buffamente.)

TRUFFALDINO

Damned be my blood! Let's go and buy him a nose!

RENZO

Oh, Truffaldino mine, three thousand miles
From this place is the city.
I'll go alone to catch the Green Bird.

TRUFFALDINO

(Aside)

Why listen to him? My task
I may not put it off. Why am I delaying?

(He goes to the Green Bird.)

Now the witch or other monsters will come out. Disasters are bound to happen. Some big monster is sure to appear.

(The Green Bird becomes menacing. Three times RENZO tries to get to him. The Green Bird touches RENZO, and RENZO is turned into a statue.)

RENZO

(As he becomes petrified.)

O, God, what do I feel? Alas what sorrow! What anguish! . . .

TRUFFALDINO

(Goes to him and clowns touching him.)

Truffaldino

Sangue de mia mader chincagliera de piazza! L'è deventà un baccalà. Duro stecchio! L'ha le chiappe de piera co fa Calmon. L'è bianco co fa un cadavere. Poareto, el me fa peccà! Ma se podesse chiappà quel bel oseleto verde, nol me farae peccà. Andarae a Venezia a averzer un casotto ...

> (Tenta di prendere l'Augellin, ma anch'egli viene toccato e pietrificato.)

O angoscia! Tristo non sarò più; di cuor mi pento; Tardi la man dà drio; xe fuora el vento!

> (L'Augellin, dopo un giro intorno ai due, sale nel suo piedestallo. I due alberi mostruosi ruotano in torno ai due e li coprono interamente. Cessa la musica e sulla foresta scende un silenzio di morte.)

SCENA V

Augello

O Ninetta, Ninetta, caccia la noia in bando;
chi vive con speranza, no muor sempre sperando
le fatali avventure a incominciar si vanno,
dalle quali dipende il nostro acerbo affanno.
Prendi il solito cibo; il mezzodì, ch'or suona,
del tuo sepolcro forse è l'ultima tua nona.

(TRUFFALDINO)

By the blood of my mother, peddling in the Piazza! Renzo's become as stiff as a salted fish! Stone dead. He has buttocks like Calmon! He's white as a corpse. Poor little wretch, it pains me! But if I could lay my hands on that little Green Bird, it wouldn't make me sad at all! I'd go to Venice, open a side show at carnival to show him off.*

> (He tries to capture the Bird, and as soon as he touches the Green Bird, he becomes petrified.)

Oh, misery! I'll no longer be naughty. Cross my heart I repent.

> (With his hand on his heart patch on his behind.)

Too late: The fart escaped!

> (The Green Bird turns and ascends his pedestal; music stops; the trees are immobile.)

SCENE V

> (The pit under the toilets.)

GREEN BIRD

O, Ninetta, stop your crying!
Not all who live in hope die in hope.
The deadly trials that will influence your destiny are about
   to start.
And it depends on your taking your nourishment.
Take the food; your last hours of captivity may soon be at an end.

---

*Boerio, G. *Dictionaria del Dialetto* Veneziano. Milano, A. Martello, 1971.

Ninetta

Ah, cara Augello, tu mi metti in forse
la mia felicità. Deh, dimmi in grazia,
quai sien queste avventure, e non tenermi
viva tremando in mille morti avvolta.

Augello

Cara Ninetta amabile, per or solo ti dico,
ch'io t'amo co' tuoi figli ... L'Orco, che m'ha cambiato,
sappi
in sul colle dell'Orco, dov'abito di stanza,
le mie parole sono di tremenda sostanza.
Lungi di là no posso dar provvidi consigli,
nè dir a tuoi gemelli posso, di chi son figli.
Sono imminenti incesti, sposalizi esecrandi ...
I padri con le figlie ... cose grandi, ma grandi
Ahi che troppo ti dissi. Volo al mio colle in fretta;
tu al buco della scaffa rimanti, spera e aspetta.

(Esce.)

Ninetta

Che intesi mai! ... ma no intesi nulla.
Superni alti consigli,
lungi dal mio consorte,
lungi dai cari figli,
diciott'anni di morte
non mi bastano ancora?
O buco, o buco della scaffa, quanto
mi terrai qui sepolta in doglia, e in pianto?

(La reggia si richiude.)

NINETTA

O, dear Bird, you put me in doubt
About happiness! Oh, tell me in pity's name,
What may be the trials? Do not keep me
Trembling while imaging a thousand deaths.

GREEN BIRD

Dear, lovable Ninetta. For you alone I tell this,
I love your two children . . . The witch that changed me
Knows
Only on the mount, where she and I live,
May my words be weighty with meaning.
Far from there, I'm not free to speak.
I'll only hint at impending incest abominable . . .
Fathers with daughters . . . Such outrageous things!
Ah, but this was a slip of the tongue. It's time I hurry
    back to the mountain.
Stay but awhile in this hole beneath the toilets. Wait with hope.

    (Exits.)

NINETTA

What did I hear! . . . Or maybe I didn't hear a thng.
Maybe it was a dream?
Far away from my consort,
Far from my dear children,
Eighteen years of a living death
In this hole are not yet sufficient?
How long in pain and tears yet will I be buried in this hole!

    (Exits.)

SCENA VI

(Sala regia)

Tartagliona

Figlio, non mi fuggir.

Tartaglia

(Tartaglia fugge dalla madre)

Signora madre,

v'ho scacciato dal cuor, più non vi soffro;

andate a farvi seppelir, ch'è tempo.

Tartagliona

O figlio d'ua strega, bricconaccio, (Rabbiosa)
becco cornuto, sonso stanca al fine,
non voglio che tu sposi una bastarda,
che non si sa chi sia. Nuore non voglio,
che sien bastarde, e diventar la nonna
di qualche discendenza vergognosa.

Tartaglia

Io non so di bastardi, o non bastarde;
so ben, che no vorreste esser mai nonna.
Sangue di Malacoda, son monarca,
voglio sposarmi a chi me pare e piace,
e voi sposate il diavol, che vi porti.

Tartagliona

O canaglia, birbante! ho inteso tutto.
Io voglio far pagamento di dote,
e farti un conto al sei per cento addosso,
che ti porterò via sin le charchesse.

SCENE VI

(Before the Royal Palace. TARTAGLIA enters running away from his mother.)

TARTAGLIONA

Son, don't run away!

TARTAGLIA

Madame, my Mother,
I've run you out of my heart; I can't stand you any longer.
It is time that you go bury yourself.

TARTAGLIONA

Oh, son of a witch, scamp,
Cuckold. I'm fed up!
I am against your marrying a bastard
Who doesn't know who she is. I don't want a daughter-in-law
Who is a bastard, nor to become grandmother
To shameful descendants.

TARTAGLIA

Bastards or no bastards,
All I know is that you don't want to be a grandmother!
By the blood of the devil Malacoda, I'm the King,
And I want to *marry* as I please.
Marry yourself to a devil who'll carry you off.

TARTAGLIONA

You knave, you scoundrel! Now I'll let it be understood:
I'll make you pay me back the dowry.
I'll attach what you own a hundred percent!
I'll snatch away even your 'britches'.

Tartaglia

Capisco, via. Questi sono consulti
di quel vostro canaglia di poeta,
che cerca farvi fare il testamento.
E voi credete, che per voi sospiri,
vecchia sena giudizio. Non vi tempo.
I vi noterò tanto d'interdetto,
vi pianterò ventiquattro conversi,
ed averò avvocati sì valenti,
che vi faran crepare sulla panca,
e quel vostro poeta pidocchioso
lo caccerò coi calci nel preterito
a scriver le conzon per la regata.

Tartagliona

Ben, ben, ci toccheremo le gambette,
leverò fra mezz'ora un vadimonio,
ed a cauzion farò bollarti il regno,
e sino i denti ch'hai nelle mascelle.
Vedrem, se allor mi porterai rispetto.
Ah, non doveva maritarmi mai:
questo è quel, che s'acquista a far dei figli.

(Piange)

Tartaglia

Andate a sequestrar Monterotondo,
e a farmi diventar un re fallito;
non bado al lagrimar dei coccodrilli.

TARTAGLIA

I get it. This comes from those sessions
With that scheming poet of yours,
Who is trying to beguile you into signing a will in his favor.
You believe that he yearns for you.
Senseless hag! I don't fear you.
I'll fix you
With twenty-four lawsuits,
And I will have such clever lawyers
That you'll burst on the bench.
And that charlatan poet of yours
I'll kick so in the ass
They'll sing songs about it at the Regata on the Redentore!

TARTAGLIONA

Well, well, we'll see who wins!
I'll institute such a law suit
You'll have to put up as bond your kingdom!
You'll be impounded up to your teeth.
We'll see then if you respect me.
I ought never to have married:
This is what I've got for a son!

    (She cries.)

TARTAGLIA

Go shut yourself up in Monterotondo.*
Cause me to be a bankrupt King!
I pay no attention to crocodile tears.

*A reference to Gozzi's play The Love of Three Oranges.

SCENA VII

Pantalone

Maestà, Maestà, cose grande, ma grande. La se reconcilia con la siora
madre: xe superflue le dissension domestiche: no gh'è più tempo.
Vegno adesso dal palazzo dei do incogniti; no i ghe xe più.
Bisogna rassegnarse; l'è za un tributo, che avemo da pagar tutti.

Tartaglia

(Disperato)

Or sarete contenta. O Giove, o Giove,
o Mercurio, o Saturno, o ciel nimico!
Vado a ficcarmi un spiedo nel bellico.

(Esce furioso)

Pantalone

Un speo in tel bonigolo! sto spettacolo, vedè.

(Esce Correndo)

Tartagliona

La cosa va pulito. O gran poeta!
Dalle minacce salva esser dovrei.

SCENA VIII

Brighella

(Entra)

I xe tutti al colle dell'Orco, maestoso mio affetto; no i doveria più
tornar a casa.

SCENE VII

PANTALONE

Majesty, Majesty, great events! But great! Reconcile yourself with Madam, your mother. It's useless to fight. There is no time for it. I come now from the palace of the two strangers! It's no longer there! We must resign ourselves. They have met with death.

TARTAGLIA

(To the Queen: he's desperate.)

Now you'll be happy!
Oh, Jove! I'm going to put my feet in my belly button.

(Exits.)

PANTALONE

His foot in his belly button! That's a sight I want to see!

(Exits running.)

TARTAGLIONA

All goes well! Oh, great poet!
I'm to be saved from all that threatened me.

SCENE VIII

BRIGHELLA

(Enters.)

They all went to the mountain in search of the Green Bird, queen of my heart. They will never come back.

Tartagliona

Così fia senza dubbio. Il re mio figlio
è per ficcarsi un spiedo nel bellico.
Palesar mi convien con mio rossore,
poeta insigne, ch'io ti sono amante.

Brighella

Grazie, che a pochi il ciel largo destina. Per altro, Maestà, la permetta, che ghe diga, la cosa no pregiudica gnente; l'è un atto de simplice prudenza. La fazza subito el so testamento.

Tartagliona

Non me parlar giammai di testamento.
Tu mi conturbi con presagi mesti.
Amami e scrivi; i tuoi dover son questi.

(Esce.)

Brighella

No gh'è remedio; no la vol sentir testamento. Xe ben vero, che sti zemelli doveria restar al colle dell'Orco, dove so, che el diavolo, sorastante alle smoderate passion umane, che va supiando da drio. Tuttavia la cabala me risponde un poco scuretto, e prevedo za che, anca se le cosse va felicemente, el povero poeta averà sempre sta resposta: "Amami, e scrivi; i tuoi dover son questi." El ciel me defenda da una patente ad honorem.

(Esce.)

SCENA IX

(Entrano Barbarina e Smeraldina.)

Barbarina

Credo quest'aura sì felice, o amica,

188

TARTAGLIONA

Doubtless it is so. The King, my son,
Is about to put his feet in his belly button.
I must confess, and I blush,
Oh, poet, that I love you.

BRIGHELLA

Thank heavens, your Majesty! Permit me to ask you, to beg you for an
act of simple prudence that will not harm you in any
way. Just make your will now — right away.

TARTAGLIONA

Never speak to me about a will!
You pester me with depressing premonitions.
Just love me and write! These are your duties.

(Exits.)

BRIGHELLA

There is no hope. She'll not draw a will in my favor. It is true, that
the twins will be at the mountain of the Ogre, where that devil ruling
over them will give them a kick in the ass. Everything about the
prophecy seems not to be much in my favor. This poet always gets
the same answer: "Love me and write poems. There are your duties."
Heaven spare me a doctorate — cum laude!

(Exits.)

SCENE IX

BARBARINA

Oh friend, I believe this happy wind

Barbarina

che ratte ci condusse, sia un prodigio
in favor del fratello.

Smeraldina

Oh, senza fallo
E fu un prodigio ancora il non cadere
e il non rompersi il collo.

Barbarina

Io qui non veggio
però il fratello. E' questo il noto colle;
quello è l'Augel Belverde. Oh, dio, vorrei
trarre il pugnal, veder se ancor risplende
o se appar sanguinoso.

Smeraldina

Eh, fatevi coraggio:
poco fa tanto ardire, ed or sì vile?

Barbarina

(Trae il pugnale, che è rosso di sangue. Si volta e vede i due
pietrificati che gli alberi mostruosi poco prima avevano messo
in vista al pubblico. S'avvicina a Renzo, mentre Smeraldina va
verso Truffaldino. Quindi la battuta:)

Oh, cielo! Oh, madre!
Morto è il fratello, ed io fui che l'uccisi.

Smeraldina

Oh, poveretta me! povero figlio!
Povera figlia! Povero marito!

(BARBARINA)

That brought us here so quickly may be an omen
In favor of my brother.

SMERALDINA

Oh, certainly
It will be a miracle if *he* didn't fall
And break his neck.

BARBARINA

I don't see
My brother here. And this is the place;
Oh, there is the Green Bird. Oh, God, I feel
As if I should draw the dagger to see if it is still bright
Or if it appears bloody.

SMERALDINA

Eh, be brave.
A moment ago you had so much daring. And now so faint-hearted?

BARBARINA

(She draws a dagger, which is red with blood. She turns and sees
the petrified RENZO and TRUFFALDINO, which the monster
trees, a moment before, had placed in view of the audience. She
draws close to RENZO, as SMERALDINA goes to TRUFFAL-
DINO.)

Oh, heavens! Oh, mother!
My brother is dead, and it was I who killed him.

SMERALDINA

Oh, poor me! Poor son!
Poor daughter! Poor husband!

Barbarina

Lasciami, Smeraldina; io più non merto
soccorso da nessuno. Più che degli altri
merito l'odio tuo. Povera donna!

Smeraldina

Barbarina, mia cara . . . mi rincresce.
Sento il cor che si spezza . . . mi dispiace.
Tutto è amor proprio, figlia; voi piangete
la morte del fratel per amor proprio.

Barbarina

A ragion mi deridi; io tutto soffro,
io disperata sono.

   (Lampi e tuono.)

Calmon

   (Appare Calmon.)
E' qui Calmon.

Smeraldina

Oh, poveretta me! qui un'altra statua.

Barbarina

Calmon, se di pietà più degna sono
se al fratel giovar posso, mi soccorri.

Calmon

Tuo fratello è perito;
gli potresti giovar, ma a grave rischio
di morte.

BARBARINA

Let me go, Smeraldina, I no longer am deserving
Of help from anyone. More than anyone,
I deserve your hate. Poor Smeraldina.

SMERALDINA

Barbarina, my dear . . . I am so sad.
My heart is breaking . . . I am so unhappy.
All is for love of self, daughter; you're crying
For the death of your brother is love of self.

BARBARINA

You are right to ridicule me. My suffering is unbearable.
I am desperate.

(Lightning and thunder.)

CALMON

(Enters.)

Calmon is here.

SMERALDINA

Oh, poor me! Another statue!

BARBARINA

Calmon, if I deserve your pity,
If I am able to come to the aid of my brother, help me!

CALMON

Your brother has perished;
You would be able to help him, but at the grave risk
Of death.

Barbarina

Bramo perire, e ridonar la vita
al fratel mio, per mia cagion perduto.

Smeraldina

Anche al marito mio, benchè era un ladro . . .

Calmon

Dall'Augel dipende
la vita del fratello, del marito
di costei. Sette passi, un piede
quattro once, un dito e un punto dei fermarti
      dall'Augel
nè alterar d'un capel questa misura, o sarai morta.
Giunta al confin, difficile a trovarsi,
dei con somma prestezza esser tu prima
a ragionare a lui. Io più non posso
se perisci giovarti. Io t'abandono.

    (Lampi e tuono. Calmon sparisce.)

Smeraldina

Diavol! Sette passi, un piede
quattro once, un dito e un punto devi fermarti
lungi da lui,
nè alterar d'un capel questa misura. Barbarina,
restiam tutte due vedove, e andiam via.

Barbarina

No, Smeraldina; al gran cimento io vado.

BARBARINA

I desire to perish and to give back life
To my brother who lost his because of me.

SMERALDINA

And I, too, for my husband — even though he was a thief . . .

CALMON

On the Green Bird depends
The life of your brother and this husband
Of yours. Seven steps, one foot
Four inches, one finger, and at this point stop before the
  Green Bird.
Don't alter by one hair this measurement, or you will die.
Having arrived right at the spot, which is difficult to
  determine,
With the greatest of quickness you must be the first
To speak to him. I won't be able,
If you fail, to help you. I take my leave of you.

(Lightning and thunder. CALMON leaves.)

SMERALDINA

What the devil! Seven steps, one foot,
Four inches, one finger and at that spot you must stop
Before him.
Not to alter by one hair this measurement! Barbarina,
Let's both remain two widows and go home.

BARBARINA

No, Smeraldina, I am going to try it.

Smeraldina

No, cara figlia.

Barbarina

Lasciami, ho risolto;
diriga il cielo i miei passi e la vista.

Smeraldina

(Queste parole segnano il ritmo dei passi di Barbarina, che
s'avvicina all'Augellino.

Adagio Barbarina; manca un passo;
mancan sol le quattr'once . . . il dito . . . il punto . . .
il punto . . . il punto solo . . . manca i punto!

(L'Augellin scende dal piedestallo e si ferma davanti a Barbarina.)

Parlate presto, è tempo; Oh, dio, che pena!

Barbarina

Augel Belverde, che tieni l'ali d'oro,
volgiti in qua: io son la tua Barbarina
che tanti monti e campagne cammina
per acquistarti, mio caro tesoro.
Augel Belverde, il mio fratel soccorri.

Augello

Da quest'ala sinistra una penna trarrai;
tocca le statue, presto; tuo fratello averai.

(Obbedisce e tocca Renzo con la piuma.)

Renzo

(Si muta da staua in uomo e abbraccia la sorella.)

SMERALDINA

No, dear daughter.

BARBARINA

Let me go! I've made up my mind;
Heaven above directs my steps and my eyes.

SMERALDINA

(This speech follows the rhythm of BARBARINA'S steps as she
advances toward the Green Bird.)

Easy, Barbarina; one step more;
Now all you lack is four inches . . . a finger . . . a dot . . . a dot . . . only a
dot . . . you need now only another dot!

(The GREEN BIRD descends from its pedestal and stops before
BARBARINA.)

Speak at once! Now! O, God, what suspense!

BARBARINA

Green Bird, with wings of gold
Fly here to me: I'm your Barbarina,
Who travels so many mountain roads
To get to you. Oh, my dear treasure.
Green Bird, come to the aid of my brother!

GREEN BIRD

From my left wing, you must take a feather;
Touch these "statues" at once; and your brother will be restored
   to you.

RENZO

(Changing from a "statue" into a man; he embraces
his sister.)

197

Renzo

Cara sorella, chi mi rende in vita?

Smeraldina

E Truffaldino, vuoi resuscitarlo?

Barbarina

(Porgendo la piuma a Smeraldina.)

Anche a lui dobbiamo ridar la vita.

Truffaldino

(Dopo esser stato toccato dalla piuma sul braccio, sulla gola, sul deretano e sullo stomaco, si trasforma da pietra in uomo.)

Ah, Ah, le gatarigole. Me pareva de esser a Venezia. Gera in gondola con una bella maschiotta.

Smeraldina

(Aprendo le braccia.)

Ah, maritino mio, vien qua che t'abbracci!

Truffaldino

Smeraldina!!!

(Fingendo di pietrificare.)

Torno de piera un'altra volta.

Smeraldina

(Prendendolo per mano.)

Andiamo, balordo.

(RENZO)

Dear sister, who gave me back my life?

SMERALDINA

(To BARBARINA.)

And Truffaldino, don't you want to revive him?

BARBARINA

(Giving the feather to SMERALDINA.)

Oh, yes, we must return him to life.

TRUFFALDINO

(After having been touched by the feather, his throat, his behind, his stomach, he is transformed from a "statue" back to a man.)

Ah, ah, it tickles. I was dreaming that I was in Venice: in a gondola with a beautiful, buxom wench.

SMERALDINA

(Taking his arm.)

Ah, my little husband, come here so I can hug you.

TRUFFALDINO

Smeraldina!!!

(Pretending to petrify again.)

I turn to stone again.

SMERALDINA

(Taking him by the hand.)

Let's go, fathead!

Tutti

Andiamo, andiamo.

(L'Augellin prende per mano Barbarina ed esce, seguito da Smeraldina e da Truffaldino.)

SCENA X

Tutti

(Esce la grotta con gli alberi mostruosi. Entrano la reggia di Tartaglia sul fondo, e la fontana al centro.)

Tartagliona

(Entrando con Brighella da sinistra e fermandosi a destra, in proscenio.)

Poeta, io mi chetai perché il volesti.

Brighella

Bisogna starghe; la mia cabala numerica responde cussì:
Se il re si sposa a Barbarina, tutte
le miserie cadran sopra di lui;
se non la sposa, il strologo Brighella
e le viscere sue son in padella.

Renzo

(Entrando da destra con Pompea e fermandosi a sinistra in proscenio.)

Mio ben; pur siam felici. Chi avria detto
che in una penna d'un Augel Belverde
fosse tanta virtude?

ALL

(In unison.)

Let's go, let's go.

(The GREEN BIRD takes BARBARINA by the hand and exits, followed by SMERALDINA and TRUFFALDINO.)

SCENE X

(The grotto with the monster trees leaves the stage. Enter upstage the backdrop of the Palace of KING TARTAGLIA and a fountain center stage.)

TARTAGLIONA

(Entering with BRIGHELLA.)

Poet, my lips are sealed because it is your wish.

BRIGHELLA

Fit the deed to the need. My numerical prophecy speaks thus:
If the King marries Barbarina, all
Misery will befall him;
If he does not marry her, the astrologer Brighella
Will have his guts in a frying pan.

RENZO

(Enters with POMPEA and stops at proscenium.)

My beloved; indeed we are happy. Who would have thought
That in the feather of a Green Bird
There would be such magic as to bring you to life?

Pompea

Io tutto deggio
all'amor vostro, e grata e amante sempre
sarò di voi fedel sposa ed umile.

Smeraldina

(Entrando da sinistra con Truffaldino. I due si dispongono,
una a sinistra e l'altro a destra, in proscenio.)

M'amerai di qui innanzi?

Truffaldino

Ah, mia diletta,
io son pieno d'idee di tenerezza
come se il primo giorno fosse questo
che tu m'hai posto al collo la cavezza.

Tartaglia

(Inseguendo Barbarina e fermandosi al centro.)

Ma, cospetto di Bacco! Barbarina,
voi m'avete chiamato a star presente
a espression d'amori e di dolcezze
per farmi dar al diavolo. Ognun gode
e il re sta a bocca secca. E' già contenta
mia madre d'esser nonna. Io non intendo
perché tiriate indietro quella mano
e ricusiate d'un monarca il letto.
Diventerò bestial come un cavallo,
e spezzerò la corda dei riguardi.

POMPEA

I owe all
To your love. Grateful and loving always,
I will be your faithful and humble wife.

SMERALDINA

(Enters left with TRUFFALDINO. The two place themselves:
SMERALDINA to the left and TRUFFALDINO to the right
of the proscenium.)

Will you love me now henceforth?

TRUFFALDINO

Ah, my delight,
My thoughts of you are full of tenderness,
As if it were the first day
That you pulled the yoke over my neck.

TARTAGLIA

(Following BARBARINA who takes a place center stage.)

Well, I'll be damned! Barbarina,
You ask me
To be witness to expressions of love and sweetness;
To make me want to give myself to the devil. Everyone enjoys
    himself,
But the King stands here with a dry mouth. Why! My mother
Seems pleased to be a grandmother. I can't understand
Why you'd withdraw your hand
And refuse the bed of a king.
I will become as wild as a horse
And kick over the traces.

Barbarina

Mio re, non vi sdegnate. E' questo il punto
di sciorre il nodo a mille cose ignote.
Truffaldin, Smeraldina, a me si rechi
dell'acqua d'or la portentosa ampolla,
il pomo e l'Augello. Io già son pronta
quando il destin lo voglia, d'essere vostra.

(Truffaldino e Smeraldina entrano da lati opposti.)

Tartaglia

Adunque il matrimonio ha da dipendere
da un pomo, da un po' d'acqua e da un uccello?
Da re d'onor che son cose ridicole.

Pantalone

Mi gh'ho la strangolariola; no posso parlar.
Chi volesse depenzer el mio interno, bisogneria
depenzer el canal del bisatto in burrasca.

(Entra l'Augellin Beverde che fa un ballo al centro. Lo segue
Smeraldina. Dall'altro lato entra Truffaldino con un pomo e
con un'ampolla d'acqua.)

Tutti

Bellissimo, bravissimi, pulito.

Tartagliona

Poeta, spero ben . . .

Brighella

Ma . . . se non la sposa, il strologo Brighella
e le viscere sue sono in padella.

BARBARINA

My King, don't be irritated. Now is the time
To undo the knot of a thousand things hitherto unknown.
Truffaldino, Smeraldina, have brought
To me the wondrous cup of golden water,
The apple, and the Green Bird. I am now ready,
When destiny wills it to be yours.

(TRUFFALDINO and SMERALDINA exit.)

TARTAGLIA

So marriage has to depend
On an apple, a little water, and a Green Bird?
For the rank of a King, this is ridiculous.

PANTALONE

I'm choking; I can't speak.
Whoever were to paint my guts,
Would have to paint a canal full of eels in a storm.

(Enter the GREEN BIRD who dances center. SMERALDINA
follows him. From the other side enters TRUFFALDINO with an
apple and a cup of water.)

ALL

Beautiful, excellent, wonderful.

TARTAGLIONA

Poet, I indeed hope . . .

BRIGHELLA

But . . . if he does not wed her, the astrologer Brighella
Will have his guts in a frying pan.

Tartaglia

Qua quella man, non aspettiamo il fulmine.

Barbarina

Pria di far ciò, mio re, l'Augel ragioni.

Tartaglia

Io non voglio sentenze di un uccello.
Datemi questa mano; io me la prendo.

Augello

Deh, fermati, m'ascolta; e inarca quelle ciglia:
non sposar Barbarina, o sposerai tua figlia.

Tartaglia

Come mia figlia? Quest'uccello è matto.

Augello

No, non son matto, no, stammi Tartaglia attento,
Toccherai con le mani il vero in un momento.
Son Renzo e Barbarina tuoi figliuoli gemelli

(Renzo e Barbarina s'abbracciano.)

per me vive Ninetta, che fu viva sepolta.
Dal buco della scaffa eccola allegra e sciolta.

(La fontana si sposta. La reggia si apre e dal "buco della scaffa" esce Ninetta che si fa avanti, quasi cieca. La reggia si richiude e la fontana ritorna al centro.)

TARTAGLIA

Your hand: let's not wait for a thunderbolt!

BARBARINA

Pray, before doing that, my King, let's hear from the Green Bird.

TARTAGLIA

I don't want speeches from a bird.
Give me your hand or I'll take it.

GREEN BIRD

Please, stop and listen to me; and listen carefully:*
Don't marry Barbarina, or you will marry your own daughter.

TARTAGLIA

How's that? My daughter? That bird is crazy.

GREEN BIRD

No, I am not crazy! No! Listen to me, Tartaglia.
The truth will come out in a minute.
Renzo and Barbarina are your twins.

    (RENZO and BARBARINA embrace.)

Thanks to me, Ninetta lives, who was buried alive.
Out from under the toilets now she is here, happy and free.

> (The fountain moves. The palace opens, and out from under the
> toilets comes forth NINETTA, almost blind. The palace
> backdrop closes, and the fountain returns to center.)

*An idiom: raise your eyebrows!

Tartagliona

Ohimè siam persi, strologo Brighella.

Brighella

Con le viscere mie nella padella.

Ninetta

Chi dall'immondo buco della scaffa
mi trasse ancora a riveder le stelle?

Tartaglia

Oh, chi vedo, chi vedo, la mia sposa!
Mi par ch'ella sia fatta un po' vecchietta,
ma non importa; sono un buon marito.
e voglio far quel che mi si conviene.
Figli . . . Ninetta . . . figli . . . son confuso!
Dunque non siete voi due cani mufferli?
Mi prende il necessario svenimento.

Pantalone

Ah, che l'ha dito, che l'aveva ben condizionai,
in quella tela incerada 'ste raise.

Augello

Nessuno dal suo posto si muova, miei padroni;
che bisogna dar fine alle trasformazioni!
Vallene Tartagliona, coi rospi, in un pantano.

(Tartagliona viene al centro.)

Si coroni il poeta, che in lei sperato ha invano.

TARTAGLIONA

Oh me. We are lost, astrologer Brighella.

BRIGHELLA

My guts *are* in the frying pan.

NINETTA

Who is taking me out of the filthy hole under the toilets
To see once more the stars?

TARTAGLIA

Oh! Whom do I see? Whom do I see? My wife!
It seems to me she has aged a bit.
But never mind; I'll be a good husband
And I'll do what is expected of me.
Children . . . Ninetta . . . children . . . I am confused!
And you're not two little puppies?
I think I'm going to faint.

PANTALONE

Now who would not say that I wrapped
Them well in that waxed linen?

GREEN BIRD

No one move from this place! Sirrahs:
I must bring about some changes!
Go, Tartagliona, with the toads, into the ditch.

(TARTAGLIONA goes center stage.)

That poet in whom you put your trust is 'crowned'!

(Brighella viene acanto di Tartagliona.

Tartagliona

Poeta, oh, dio, mi cambio in una rana.

(Si porta al viso una maschera da rana.)

Brighella

Caro idol mio, mi cambio in un somaro.

(Si leva il cappello a punta e sotto spuntano due orecchie d'asino. Quindi i due escono mimando i due animali.)

Tartaglia

Oh, poffar Bacco, la regina madre
cambiata in rana che va via!

Augello

Attenti, miei signori, all'ultimo portento.
Son re di Terradombra:

(Si sposta a lato della fontana e si nasconde. Dal lato opposto entra il Re di Terradombra che continua la buttuta.)

in augello fatato
come sa l'uditorio, fui dall'Orco cambiato.
Ora tutto è compiuto; finisco la mia sorte
abbraccio Barbarina, la piglio per consorte.

Calmon

E' qui Calmon.

(Lampi e tuono. Calmon entra.)

(BRIGHELLA goes to the side of TARTAGLIONA.)

TARTAGLIONA

(Wearing the mask of a frog.)

Poet, Oh, God, I am changed into a frog.

BRIGHELLA

(Removing his hat reveals donkey ears.)

Oh, my idol I am changed into an ass!

(The two exit, making their respective animal sounds.)

TARTAGLIA

Well, by God! The Queen Mother
Has changed into a frog and off she hops.

GREEN BIRD

Take heed, all, to the final miracle;
I am the King of Terrandombra!:

(He goes behind the fountain; from the opposite side he comes
forth as the King of Terrandombra.)

Into a bird I was changed,
As you have heard, by an envious witch.
Now all has ended. I finish my tale,
I embrace Barbarina, making her my consort.

CALMON

Here is Calmon.

(Thunder and lightning.)

Tartaglia

Ancora trasformazioni!

Truffaldino

La statua dalla voce de manza.

Calmon

O Renzo, filosofo da strapazzo,
questo naso me lo vuoi restaurare?

Renzo

(Uscendo dal gruppo.)

Truffaldino, una scala e due scalpelli.

(Truffaldino porta in scena una scala, vi sale e scalpella il naso
di Calmon che dà tre gridi, cui ne seguono altrettanti del
gruppo. Quindi Renzo gli assesta sulla maschera un lungo
naso aquilino. Tutti esclamano un lungo "Oh!!" di meraviglia. Tutti si dispongono a coppie intorno a Calmon. Le luci si
spengono e cala il sipario.)

TARTAGLIA

Another transformation!

TRUFFALDINO

The statue with the voice of a bull.

CALMON

Oh, Renzo, puny philosopher,
When are you to restore this nose?

RENZO

(Standing off from the group.)

Truffaldino, a ladder and two chisels.

(TRUFFALDINO carries onstage a ladder; he climbs it. He sculpts a nose for CALMON, who utters three cries of pain, each followed by sighs from the group. RENZO places on the mask of CALMON a long aquiline nose. All exclaim a long "Ohhh!!" of wonder, as they group themselves about CALMON. Lights dim and the curtains close.)

SELECTED BIBLIOGRAPHY

Bentley, Eric. *The Genius of the Italian Theater*. New York: New American Library. 1964.

Bentley, Eric. *The Classic Theater. Volume I* (Italian Plays). Doubleday Anchor, 1958.

Drake, W. A. *Memoirs of Carlo Goldoni*. New York: Alfred Knopf, 1926.

DuChartre, Pierre Louis. *The Italian Comedy*. New York: Dover Publications, Inc., 1966.

DuChartre, Pierre Louis. *La Commedia dell'Arte*. Paris: Librairie de France, 1925.

Goldoni, Carlo. *Dalle Maschere Alla Commedia*. Venice: Carlo Ferrari, 1957.

Rosi, Luigi. *I Comici Italiani*. Florence: Fracesco Lumachi, 1905.

Smith, Winifred. *Italian Actors of the Renaissance*. New York: Coward-McCann, Inc., 1930.

MATERIALS AND BACKGROUND

Barzini, L. *The Italians*, New York: Athenium, 1977.

Barzini, L. *The Europeans*, New York: Simon and Schuster, 1983.

Goethe, J. W. (tr. by Auden, W. H. and Mayer, E.) *Italian Journey*. New York: Schocken Books, 1968.

Mitchell, John D. "In Search of Commedia dell'Arte." *Players Magazine*. New York: January, 1963.

Poli, Giovanni. "Commedia dell'Arte — A Renewal of the Theatre". *Players Magazine*. New York: January, 1963.

Poli, Giovanni. "Commedia dell'Arte — Its Application Now". *Equity Magazine*. New York: Winter, 1963.

MUSIC

Fleetwood Singers *Italian Music* (12-58) Lyr. 775.

Goldoni. *Commedia dell'Arte Melodramma*. Stereoletteraria STI 26.

CPSIA information can be obtained at www.ICGtesting.com
Printed in the USA
BVOW060418120112

280355BV00003B/2/P